"This book is packed, racked, stacked, and organized for busy language educators. As a decade-long world language teacher, I know the value of practical and engaging language activities. In this book, you can literally turn to any page and get something for class tomorrow. True language teachers will appreciate the book's organization into language domains: listening, speaking, reading, and writing. And the cherry on top? It all comes from Brent Warner, someone I have admired for tech-inspired language learning for years. You can't go wrong with this book."

　　—Matt Miller, Creator of *Ditch That Textbook*, Author, Speaker, and Spanish Teacher

"I've followed Brent Warner for years, so I'm delighted to have this book of activities. Brent makes edtech so practical that I could begin implementing suggestions immediately. Any teacher of multilingual learners will love this resource!"

　　—Dr. Carol Salva, Lead Consultant, Seidlitz Education

"As a longtime language educator and someone deeply immersed in AI in education, I thoroughly enjoyed reading *Edtech for Multilingual Learners*. Brent Warner doesn't just talk about edtech; he focuses on multilingual learners in every recommendation he makes. What I love about this book is that it's full of intentionally designed strategies that move beyond translation and vocabulary apps. It's about helping students find their voice, build confidence, and thrive throughout their learning journey. Every activity is grounded in strong pedagogy and aligned with the ISTE Standards, making this book a true bridge between tech innovation and effective teaching practice. A great resource for language educators seeking to embrace emerging technology and support student learning!"

　　—Dr. Rachelle Dené Poth, Spanish, French, and STEAM Educator,
　　　Consultant, ISTE Author

"I am pleased to recommend Brent's insightful book of practical tips! Combining encouragement, examples, and clever commentary, Brent elucidates savvy choices and possible classroom applications based on his own explorations and DIESOL interviews. While many caring educators are learning by doing and experimenting with different AI tools to engage students, accelerate English language acquisition, and increase learner autonomy, few possess Brent's intense curiosity or depth of edtech knowledge."

　　—Eric H. Roth, Master Lecturer, The American Language Institute at the
　　　USC Dana and David Dornsife College of Letters, Arts & Sciences, University
　　　of Southern California

EDTECH FOR MULTILINGUAL LEARNERS

48 Fun and Flexible Activities for Every Classroom

Brent G Warner

International Society for Technology in Education
ARLINGTON, VIRGINIA

Edtech for Multilingual Learners
48 Fun and Flexible Activities for Every Classroom
Brent Warner

Director of Books and Journals: *Emily Reed*
Senior Acquisitions Editor: *Valerie Witte*
Editor: *Stephanie Argy*
Copy Editor: *Joanna Szabo*
Proofreader: *Rachael Phillips*
Indexer: *Kento Ikeda*
Book Design and Production: *Kim McGovern*
Cover Design: *Christina DeYoung*

Library of Congress Cataloging-in-Publication Data

Names: Warner, Brent, author.
Title: Edtech for multilingual learners : 48 fun and flexible activities
   for every classroom / Brent Warner.
Description: Arlington, Virginia : International Society for Technology in
   Education, [2025] | Includes bibliographical references and index.
Identifiers: LCCN 2024052841 (print) | LCCN 2024052842 (ebook) | ISBN 9798888370506
(paperback) | ISBN 9798888370483 (epub) | ISBN 9798888370490 (pdf)
Subjects: LCSH: Multilingual education—Effect of technological innovations on. |
   Educational technology. | Creative activities and seat work. |
   English language—Study and teaching—Foreign speakers—Activity programs. |
   Language acquisition—Computer-assisted instruction.
Classification: LCC LC3715 .W37 2025 (print) | LCC LC3715 (ebook) | DDC
   370.117/5—dc23/eng/20250131
LC record available at https://lccn.loc.gov/2024052841
LC ebook record available at https://lccn.loc.gov/2024052842

First Edition
ISBN: 979-8-88837-050-6

Ebook version available
ISBN EPUB: 979-8-88837-048-3
ISBN PDF: 979-8-88837-049-0

Printed in the United States of America

Cover Art: © 2025
Inside Art: © 2025

ISTE® is a registered trademark of the International Society for Technology in Education.

About ISTE

The International Society for Technology in Education (ISTE) is home to a passionate community of global educators who believe in the power of technology to transform teaching and learning, accelerate innovation and solve tough problems in education.

ISTE inspires the creation of solutions and connections that improve opportunities for all learners by delivering: practical guidance, evidence-based professional learning, virtual networks, thought-provoking events and the ISTE Standards. ISTE is also the leading publisher of books focused on technology in education. For more information or to become an ISTE member, visit iste.org. Subscribe to ISTE's YouTube channel and connect with ISTE Facebook and LinkedIn.

Related ISTE Titles

How to Teach AI: Weaving Strategies and Activities into Any Content Area
by Rachelle Dené Poth (2024)

AI in the Classroom: Strategies and Activities to Enrich Student Learning
by Nancye Blair Black (2023) (jump start guide)

To see all books available from ISTE, please visit iste.org/books.

About the Author

 Brent Warner is an award-winning professor at Irvine Valley College in Southern California. His work focuses on integrating technology and innovation into the language learning process. He works with teachers and organizations across the globe to provide practical advice for helping English Language Learners take advantage of tech to help them communicate more clearly. He blogs about technology integration in the ESOL classroom for TESOL International Association, and he is the co-host of The DIESOL Podcast (DIESOL.org), focusing on innovation in ESOL, as well as The Higher EdTech Podcast (TheHigherEdTechPodcast.com), focusing on tech for teachers in college and university settings. He gets just as excited talking about coffee as he does about pedagogy, so be careful bringing up the two topics together around him.

Acknowledgments

Publisher's Acknowledgments

ISTE gratefully acknowledges the contributions of the following:

ISTE Standards reviewers: Lisa Berghoff, April Burton, Jana Gerard, Courtney Waldmann.

Manuscript reviewers: Jacqueline Liesch, Amanda Nguyen, Ilene Winokur.

Author's Acknowledgments

There are far too many people who helped me along on this journey to give credit to everyone, but I want to acknowledge the people whose support, direct conversations, and collaborations made this book possible: Ixchell Reyes, Rebecca Beck, Jeff Wilson, Susan Akhavan, Brooke Bui, Eric H. Roth, Tim VanNorman, Stephanie Argy, Valerie Witte, Tomiko Breland, Sarah Sahr, Cate Tolnai, Nichole Carter, Ed Campos Jr., Brian Briggs, Ryan O'Donnell, Brooke Warner, and of course, my wife Miyuki, who has supported me from the beginning.

Finally, thank you to *you*, the intrepid teachers who have come to my presentations, joined my classes, and followed along with my work online. Every message has encouraged me to keep exploring and sharing!

Dedication

To my dad, Nick Warner, who always supported my nerdy tech endeavors.

To my mom, Gail Warner, who showed me that willingness to try something new can get you pretty dang far in life.

Contents

READING

WRITING

VOCABULARY

EDTECH FOR MULTILINGUAL LEARNERS

PRONUNCIATION

APPENDIX

Preface

Computer Assisted Language Learning (**CALL**) has long been a recognized subfield of language acquisition studies, but only in recent years has it made the jump from "geeks tucked away in a far-off corner of the conference" to "Oh, everybody needs to know this!" The shift comes at the convergence of many points: the ubiquity of mobile devices, the ever-dropping cost of computers, a social shift in priorities with generational change, a clearer understanding of what's possible after being forced to use tech during COVID lockdowns, and more. For those of us who have been touting the benefits of tech integration in the language learning process, there's probably a little "I've been telling you … ," but once we get over ourselves there's a lot more "Look at this cool thing I want to show you!"

This book is a collection of cool things I want to show you.

I am a college professor, so people are often surprised that I spend the majority of my professional development at conferences for K–12 teachers. Higher ed professors are getting better at incorporating practical pedagogy and edtech, but I find that too many academic conferences are focused on presenting the findings of hyper-niche studies involving six subjects and outcomes with recommendations to study the topic more. My friends in primary and secondary, meanwhile, are locked in on trying to find activities, tools, and techniques they can bring into class the following Monday. While research will always be vital to the field, my intention is always to move it from theory to practice, exploring ways we can apply the research to meaningful and engaging activities for our students.

This book is aspirational, not prescriptive. While my goal is to provide you with a guide to activities that incorporate tech in the language learning classroom, it is not to tell you how to teach or to presume that I know what's best for your students or your classroom. You will find that many of the activities are flexible, and none are time-indicated. In other words, these activities are not meant to be seen as a soufflé recipe that needs to be followed precisely and closely, lest everything fall apart. Instead, you are meant to treat them like a recipe for a stew in a slow cooker: Add the parts you like, discard the parts you don't, replace the things that you don't have with something you do, and run it as long or as short as you need.

It's long been a dream of mine that CALL moves away from being a special interest area for a subset of teachers and instead becomes a system of support that is second nature for all language teachers. This shift is already taking place, and my hope is that this book helps contribute to that move.

Cheers to the explorers!

—*Brent Warner*

INTRODUCTION

While I hope that this book serves as a valuable resource to English language teachers across the world, it's worth noting that English learners are not served only in English Language Development (ELD) classes. According to the US Department of Education, "English learners (ELs) are one of the fastest growing student demographics in the United States, and are a diverse group, representing over 400 different language backgrounds" (US Department of Education, 2019). Meanwhile, the National Center for Education Statistics tell us that in the United States, 10.6% of enrolled students are ELs, and some states like California and Texas are on course to double that number (National Center for Education Statistics, 2024). These numbers represent statistics only in the US. Looking across the globe, we can see even more need for direct support for teachers to integrate technology for ELs. The 48 activities in this book are meant to help you do that, whether you're just starting to play with more tech tools or if you've got an established routine for digitally enhanced learning. I hope they serve you well.

About the Resources

As you will see, every chapter of this book comes with a QR code and a link to relevant resources. It only takes a few seconds to create an account, and anyone who bought the book will get access to the full set of resources for the book—absolutely free.

brentgwarner.com/register/

I've provided a **slide deck** for every activity in the form of Google Slides to keep things as universally accessible as possible. The intention was to make it as close to plug and play as I could, so you can simply pull up the slide deck and walk the students through your chosen activity. You are also able to create your own copy of each slide deck and edit your copy to your heart's content, so if the way I set it up needs fine-tuning for your classroom needs, please copy, delete, edit, and add as needed.

Additionally, many of the resources include sample activities from the primary tool I suggested for that activity. In all cases where possible, I've also made the sample activities replicable so you can only be a click away from your own copy to use as you please.

Finally, since edtech moves so quickly, having the resources online will allow me to update content to better match the changing availability of tools. If one of the providers closes shop, as we see too often, I'll be able to go in and make alternate suggestions.

I hope you find that the resource section explodes the value of this book from "excellent" to "astronomical."

A Guide to Links

While this book is focused on pedagogical activities, you can't really talk edtech without sharing links to resources. Ebooks make it easy enough to provide direct links, but printed material still requires us to take some action to access recommended tools and materials. In order to simplify the process, you will see three different types of links.

Same Name URLs

When a resource has a URL that matches its name with a .com, .org, or other domain name directly tagged onto the end, I've written the name of the resource as its website.

For example: iste.org

Simple Links

Some resources have links that are easy enough to remember and type into your browser. If they're only one subfolder or subdomain away, I included the link in parentheses.

For example: (iste.org/standards)

Edushare.ing for Longer Links

Some links have complicated structures or multiple subfolders or subdomains. To accommodate these, I created https://edushare.ing. This is an open-source URL shortener I built to help teachers share links. Many of the best-known URL shorteners are starting to slide in advertisements, so to eliminate that kind of tomfoolery, I built my own. This guarantees that you won't be tracked, redirected in weird ways, or advertised to when you just want to go to a certain resource.

E.g. iste.org/learning-library/books would be (edushare.ing/istebooks)

By the way, I also made Edushare.ing public facing and open access, so if you've got long links (I'm thinking online **slide decks**, etc.), and you're a bit leery of the ways the prominent URL shorteners are redirecting your traffic, please feel free to use Edushare.ing to your heart's content. Just a small gift as a thank you for all the teachers out there trying to share out and help one another.

Glossary of Terms

Terms that appear in **bold** when they're introduced later in the book are in this glossary.

1:1 Classroom. A room where every student has a device (computer/tablet) for themselves.

CALL. Computer Assisted Language Learning. A subfield of language acquisition focused on using technology to help language learners.

slide deck. A generalized term for a given file used for presentations. Often referred to as a PowerPoint, PPT, slides, etc.

word processor. Any software program used primarily for writing. Commonly recognized through programs like Microsoft Word or Google Docs, though there are many choices out there.

podcatcher. This is a program or app with the specific goal of playing podcasts. While many podcast listeners stick with the basic version they got on their computer or phone, there's a whole world of custom-built podcatchers. If you're looking for a "which is better" argument to get into with edtech nerds, podcatchers aren't a bad place to start.

SIDE NOTES: Most chapters have a side note or two, indicated with this megaphone icon. These side notes may be tips, things to be aware of, variations, or anything else that I thought was worth sharing but that didn't quite fit into the flow of the activity. They're not necessary to run the activities, but I hope you find them helpful nonetheless.

open source. A software program whose code is made to be transparent and fully accessible to the users. Most teachers don't have the time to develop their own programs, but open source software is generally considered to be positive because anyone can go in and see if there's malicious coding. If you're going to start experimenting with lesser-known products, seeing that it's open source is typically a good sign.

synchronous classes. Classes where students gather together and work at the same time. These can be traditional in-person classes or online via platforms like Zoom.

asynchronous classes. Classes run online where students are free to complete the work at any time that suits their schedule. Students will typically watch videos and do readings in place of a live lecture.

File Types

We won't go into the long and storied history of file types, especially those around images, but needless to say we've all felt frustration around trying to move images around from one program to another only to find it no longer displays. It seems that every company is trying to make their own high-resolution/small-file-size image, typically ending in forcing us, the end users, to find a way to convert it back to the classics:

- **JPG.** The most common image file type. Useful for displaying online or for printing, but remember that JPGs with small file sizes do not print well.

- **PNG.** The preferred file type for images you'll only use online. PNGs also allow for transparent backgrounds so you can fit them into a thoughtfully designed document with ease.

- **GIF.** These are graphics which are most commonly used these days as animated images pulled from pop culture. This is absolutely, positively pronounced "gif" and anybody who argues the point is a bad, bad person.

AI Terms

- **LLM (Large Language Model).** This is a type of AI that is specifically trained to recognize, interpret, and generate text. When I say large, I mean LARGE. Most companies are hesitant to spill the beans, but some estimate the dataset of the old ChatGPT 3.0 model to be between 570 GB to 45 TB. To put that in perspective, it would take the average human about 500 days to read through 1 GB of text if they didn't take the time to eat, sleep, or binge all those British police dramas instead of grading students' papers I was supposed to.

- **Prompts.** We're living in a world with a low tolerance for trends, especially when it comes to tech. There are already people out there hyping the "end of prompt engineering" as quickly as the same people hyped it as the next big thing. When I talk about prompts, I'm simply referring to the words that you use to ask a chatbot to do something. Regardless of the semantics, building quality prompts is simply the skill of being a good communicator. As teachers, we do our students a great service if we teach them that better language skills lead to better prompts.

- **Chatbot.** Throughout the book you will see me refer to "chatbots" as a catchall for most AI platforms. If you can type into it and it responds to you automatically, it's a chatbot. At the time of publication, popular chatbots include ChatGPT, Microsoft Copilot, Google Gemini, Claude, and Perplexity, among others.

Linguistic Terms

While this book may be used by many language teachers, the hope is that other content-area teachers can see the value of these activities for their own language learners and apply them in history, science, and all the other classes out there—yes, even math! (And if you're a math teacher who uses any of these ideas, please let me know!) With that in mind, I'll share a few linguistic terms that might come up, but for the most part, I'm trying to drop the language acquisition lingo.

- **L1.** A student's first language.

- **L2.** A student's second language, though this starts to get fraught with arguments about how many languages a student speaks and other well-meaning concerns from us language nerds who may be a little too concerned with semantics. Typically, L2 is the language you're teaching your language learners in.

- **Prescriptivism.** An approach to linguistics that is heavily focused on using language "correctly." This can be valuable for teaching grammar or pronunciation that causes confusion if not carefully constructed.

- **Descriptivism.** An approach to linguistics that focuses much more on how language is actually used rather than the rules (which may or may not be followed in the real world). This can be valuable to help students focus on fluency over accuracy. Note that both prescriptivism and descriptivism are on a spectrum, and it's a good idea to take an open-minded approach to both. Sometimes we need the rules, and other times we're just being nitpicky because of our own biases around language.

About AI

You can't open an app on your phone without being inundated with think pieces, tutorials, apocalyptic doomsayers, or bright-eyed futurists talking about artificial intelligence. I personally love it and fear it, embrace it and push it away. I believe that the only reasonable approach is a combination of hopeful curiosity and healthy skepticism. I experiment with it a lot, and overall I tend to be optimistic about its use in language learning. I also tend to question what will happen to the world of language teaching because of it. Pluses and minuses, all together.

AI Is Powerful.

If you're not experimenting with how AI can help your students learn a language, it's time to get on the boat! There's an endless world of creative opportunities here, and I share some ideas throughout the book of ways you can play with it. The speed at which it is improving is hard to keep track of, so just remember to take baby steps. You'll get there!

For those who are looking to experiment with AI in language learning, please visit AIforMLLs.com, where we share explorations and discoveries. It's also an open invitation to post, so please send me a message there if you'd like to share your own experiences.

AI Makes Mistakes

Despite the fact that I'm encouraging you to explore AI, it's important to know that different versions of it have different strengths and weaknesses. While they may look similar on the surface, the updates are regular and can be significant. Make sure to check how well it completes assignments before you give them to students, so you can be aware of problem areas.

Why Isn't This Book an AI for Language Learners Book?

Artificial intelligence is a wonderful and powerful (as well as sometimes fraught and problematic) part of the edtech world. But as much as it may be on people's minds, AI falls under the edtech umbrella, and not the other way around. It is great at generating content and helping us explore creative approaches, but it (currently) struggles with one of the great strengths traditional computer software has always had: consistency and reliability. If I made a very basic multiple-choice quiz using any traditional edtech tool, I could safely rely on a very predictable outcome with accurate assessments. Any mistakes would likely come from me as the teacher who set up the quiz, and not the quizzing platform. AI, on the other hand, doesn't have "logic" as we understand it. **Chatbots** are simply predicting the next most likely word (or part of a word) based on the request made of it. Think of it as the difference between going to McDonald's and having a personal chef. McDonald's entire goal is to ensure consistency across the planet, so no matter where you go, you'll always know that the Big Mac you ordered will be the Big Mac you desired. The personal chef has a much wider repertoire, but depending on their mood, the ingredients available to them on that day and what they understand about your preferences, you may end up with wildly different meals from day to day. Neither of these are right or wrong (I can hear some people screaming at me that absolutely one of these is wrong, but you get my point), it's a question of what you're looking for at the moment.

This book is about using tech to engage students in the process of language learning. AI is a part of that, but it will only be treated as a part. As teachers, we need both the consistency of traditional software and the unpredictable nature of AI to best engage our students. With that in mind, AI-based activities are included as a given. They are peppered throughout the book with the same goals as the rest of the activities: to engage students and to help you see some ways of working with tech that you might not have considered before. That said, I do write and share a LOT about AI outside of this book, so if you want to keep up with that side of things, please feel free to join my mailing list or find me across the internet, starting at BrentGWarner.com.

The Fundamentals of Edtech

You don't have to be an expert on technology to use this book. Still, as we're already well into the 21st century, I do have some broad-level ideas people will need to know in general:

Assumptions

Throughout this book I'm making a number of assumptions about your technology setup. While I recognize that the world does not equally have access to the same tech, this book is focused on the goal of using widely available tech to increase engagement, track work, and develop language skills. Not every activity in this book requires the most modern tech or that every student has a computer with all the bells and whistles, but in order to avoid repetition and writing accommodations for every situation, I'm making a few assumptions about mindset, digital competency, and tech.

Mindset

Nobody writing any book for teachers can fairly claim to cover all needs or understand the dynamics of each campus and classroom. My hope is that you'll view these activities as inspirational and not as **prescriptive**. My assumption is that you're looking at these activities and making changes to suit the needs of your particular classroom. Perhaps you'll come across an activity that requires computers for every student, but you don't have a **1:1 classroom**. In such a situation, it's worth asking yourself if everybody can do the work on their phones, or on a few shared laptops. These are the types of situations where flexibility is key. If you ever find yourself wondering "I wonder if it's OK to do _____ instead," the answer is a resounding "Yes!"—so give it a try!

Digital Competency

We live in a digital world. There's simply no doubt about it, and things are not slowing down on this front. In a 2023 report on the digital divide, the National Skills Coalition argued that across industries, 92% of jobs require digital skills (Bergson-Shilcock et al., 2023). Using technology in the classroom is not just about shiny toys and blinky screens. Building an understanding of how to use online tools and communicate to be prepared to live in the modern world is a cornerstone of the ISTE Standards.

Tech

With that clarified (and it really is more important than anything else!), let's look at the basic tech I'm assuming you and your students have.

Internet

- Students have reliable access to the internet at home and at school.

- Internet speeds are high enough to allow for uploading and downloading of video as needed.
- All devices and setups below have access to the internet.

Computers

- Students have access to laptops or desktops on campus. Ideally, classrooms have options for 1:1 setups (one computer per student), but sometimes this requires going to a computer lab or for students to bring their own computers.
- Students have access to a laptop or desktop at home.
- Any computer students have access to includes a camera and a microphone.

Mobile Devices

- Students have access to a smartphone or tablet. Any mobile device students have access to includes a camera and a microphone.

Classroom

- Physical classrooms are "Connected Classrooms," meaning they typically have the following resources:
  - a teacher station with a teacher's own computer (also with a camera and a microphone)
  - a projector that can display the content on the teacher's computer screen
  - speakers to play audio to the classroom
- Online classrooms in the context of this book refer to **synchronous** classes, which the teacher is presenting live to their students through platforms like Zoom, Google Meet, or Microsoft Teams. Regardless of the platform, you will typically have the following resources:
  - a fully functional computer with a working camera and microphone
  - the ability to share your screen, so that it serves as an online projector
  - the ability to play audio from your computer through the meeting platform
- I'll still clarify what materials I'm suggesting for each activity, but remember that your needs and resources are invariably different from your fellow teachers in different districts, states, or countries, and that's part of what makes this all so interesting to figure out!

Software

One of the perils of writing an edtech book is that companies go out of business, get bought out, rebrand, or (infamously in the case of Google's suite of tools) get shut down when teachers start to love them. On top of the things that happen to the companies, they also change their pricing plans or shift availability. While we'd all love a world where we could wave a golden ticket saying, "I'm a TEACHER!" and simply get access to whatever we want, edtech companies do not tend to bend to our whims.

Still, I'm assuming that the recommendations I give here are taken only as suggestions with a firm understanding that I cannot see into the future. Free software may become paid, and (less likely) paid software may become free. Likewise, freemium models may change what you get access to. Finally, as language teachers many of us are working from different places around the world, and licensing, firewalls, and more may be very different from country to country. Please take the time to look into the recommended software and if you need more hints and alternatives, check out the ELT Toolkit I built for the TESOL International Association at www.tesol.org/elt-toolkit.

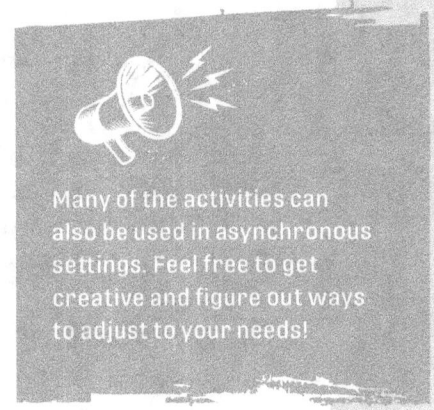

Many of the activities can also be used in asynchronous settings. Feel free to get creative and figure out ways to adjust to your needs!

For more on pricing, please see "Cost of Services."

There's also the question of whether you should use your school email address to make accounts. If you're very confident you aren't going to be leaving your school anytime soon, yes. Your school accounts are much more likely to conform to school requirements. But if you tend to switch schools from year to year, or need to move semi-regularly, you will need to determine for yourself if using a custom email account (YourName-Teacher@gmail.com or something to that effect) is the right choice for you.

Hardware

While there are other interesting gadgets and doodads that I'd love more people to experiment with in the classroom, I'm avoiding talking about anything but the most ubiquitous of resources. In short, we're talking about the computers, the mobile devices, and the classroom setup as mentioned above. While it might be (definitely would be) cool, you will not suddenly see an activity in this book that requires a $20,000 robot on wheels or even a class set of throwable microphones. Still, if you're getting grants and finding uses for those things, share it with me online at @BrentGWarner because I do want to see how you're using them with your language learners!

Sharing and Collecting Digital Documents

Sharing and collecting digital documents can be different across platforms and resources. There are typically a few things that need to be considered:

- Will every student have their own copy of the document, or will everybody work together on one large, shared document?

- Is the document distributed through an LMS (Canvas, Schoology, Google Classroom, etc.) or shared directly by the teacher through links?

- How are students expected to return the documents? Submitting inside the LMS? Sending a link back? Showing the completed work directly to the teacher by calling them over to look at it?

As there are so many different approaches and not all schools run tech solutions in the same way, this book assumes you can work with your instructional technologist, tech coach, Teacher on Special Assignment (TOSA), or equivalent on campus to make sure you can distribute and collect documents in the best way.

Things You Need to Know How to Do

- Manage your LMS. More and more, we're seeing students holding their teachers to higher standards of expectations in the way they control the distribution of information online. In other words, you've gotta get a lock on how to use your Learning Management System. While it would be nice if I could give full instructions on how to manage your LMS, the variety of systems and individual ways to make features work is beyond the capacity of any one resource and would only leave a page or two for the real goal of this book. This book is designed to provide activities that you can use regardless of whether your school dictates that you use Blackboard, Moodle, Canvas, Google Classroom, or any of the other systems available. If you're not comfortable with your LMS, but you find yourself wanting to use some of the activities in this book, I suggest you show the activity you'd like to try to your instructional technologist (or a nerdy teacher friend), who should be able to get you started. This will also be a good way to help you become more comfortable with your LMS.

  - Things you need to know how to do inside your LMS:

    - Distribute documents to your students. This may be in the form of a single shared document for your whole class, to small groups, or to individual students.

    - Collect assignments. Do you want students to send you links to their outside work? Should they upload files for you to access? What's the process for doing that? No one solution is best for everyone, though I tend to be of the mindset that fewer clicks and less need to organize files on my part before I get started on feedback makes me a much happier camper. Note that on most assignments, I don't provide you with techniques on how students should submit their work, so please make sure you figure out the best way for you to receive their assignments before you start the activity.

- Embed HTML. I know this sounds a little scary, but usually it's just copying and pasting.

- Connect outside apps. You may have heard some of the techy people on campus talk about an LTI. This stands for Learning Tools Interoperability and is basically a fancy way to say "bringing an app into your LMS." In the activities in this book, I don't specifically ask you to connect apps into your LMS, but you may find that doing so rather than linking students to outside websites all the time creates an easier workflow for you in the long run.

○ Record yourself. Before we get to the technical side, let's talk about the human side of why this is important. Many teachers try to save time by trying to find a YouTube video that teaches a concept they're covering in class, but this is missing a key opportunity to connect with students. The more students hear your voice and understand *your* way of explaining things, the easier it will be for them to form a bond with you and to learn from you when you're working together. Hopefully part of the reason you became a teacher is because you believe that you can help students, so lean into it!

- Types of recordings you need to be able to do:

  - Video: This may be a quick and dirty video recorded on the fly right inside your LMS, or it may be a full-on production made through a system like Camtasia (techsmith.com/camtasia). Don't worry—there are a LOT of options for teachers that land in the middle, including ScreenPal.com, Screencastify.com, Loom.com, and more. And if, by chance, my opinion on which tools to use matters to you, check out the companion ELT Toolkit, built to help teachers out at tesol.org/elt-toolkit.

  - Audio: There's a whole world of audio-related tech, but there's surprisingly little to work with for beginners or even intermediate users. Many teachers choose video options and simply turn off the camera (a fine choice, by the way!), but after years of podcasting, I'm a bit of a purist, and I personally will go to the effort to record audio either right on the web with something super simple like Vocaroo.com or online-voice-recorder.com, or step it up a bit and record in a dedicated app like GarageBand (edushare.ing/GarageBand) on Mac or Audacity (audacityteam.org) across platforms (free and **open source**, so they'll always have a piece of my heart).

Cost of Services

One persistent issue with edtech tools is the tug-of-war between teachers, who are often underfunded and already pay for too many supplies on their own, and companies who need to pay the bills and hire programmers to make their visions for students come to life. Or put more simply: Teachers want free services, while companies want to charge.

There are a lot of dynamics at play when it comes to costs involved, and debating the merits and pitfalls of all these dynamics isn't going to change the fact that most teachers will have to pick and choose what they pay for, if they can afford to pay anything at all.

Most of the tools in this book try to keep an option for teachers to explore or work with a product without having to pay for it. That said, companies change how they work, so let's look at my best effort to keep things from sending you into financial despair.

Straight-Up Free

This is the most ideal. You will notice that I focus on a number of tools by major companies like Google, Microsoft, Canva, etc. This is because they offer their services for free, and they generally have the resources to continue updating and offering expansions. This doesn't mean these are perfect companies, and yes—the old adage that if something is free, then you are the product is worth keeping in mind. Still, at the end of the day, most of us are just trying to help our students, and free is free.

Also remember that there's a whole world of open-source tools made by people (tinkerers, teachers, and more) who just wanted to create something because they saw a need, and they figured that they could create it. These are often not as shiny or polished, but they are my absolute favorite kind of tool and they represent the best of what humanity and the internet have to offer. Most of these sites have a tiny donation button, and I do my best to send some money their way as a thanks for their efforts.

Freemium

Some cases follow the freemium model, where you get a limited number of features for free. In the cases where the tools have a freemium model, I've done my best to focus on what you can do with the freely available features, and not on features you have to pay to get. This can get sticky as some services rotate their free features, which can be frustrating if you haven't checked in for a bit. More frustrating still is when companies begin to bottleneck their free features, starting off with a decent number of useable features then slowly shrinking it down to three, then two, then one ... all while paying lip service to the idea that "we will always have a free option." Mmhmm. We see you.

Trial Service

A lot of companies love to "give" teachers 30 days, or 60 days, or 90 days of full access to their platform. Here's my problem with free trials: They require you to induct your students into the use of the tool, making you spend a lot of time getting used to it, and just when things seem to be working, it cuts you off—right in the middle of the semester! To me, that's a hard no. If I can't trial it for at least a full semester, it's not something I want to invest my time and energy into. I haven't included anything in this book that asks you to sign up for a service just long enough to do the activity and then run out the door. That said, I have found it can be effective to reach out to companies with a limited free trial and explain to them that you need a full semester.

Premium / Plus / Enterprise

Finally, we get to the bank breakers: paying full price for a product. To be clear, I'm all in favor of paying for useful services. Sometimes it's just a simple question of math: If this product is $8 a month and it's going to save me four hours a week, do I consider my time more valuable than 50 cents an hour? OK, then perhaps this is a worthwhile investment. Still, these things can add up, and a lot of companies are betting that you'll forget you have a recurring payment going (there are VERY few single payment options these days, much to my chagrin), so you have to go through and clear out your subscriptions every once in a while.

At the end of the day, though, I'm doing my best to avoid activities that require a premium service. This does, admittedly, limit some of the options I share. In fact, it means that there are some really cool activities you could do, and that the technology is there for, but that I didn't include because there are only one or two services that let you do it, and they're behind paywalls. If you have some funds or if your school is willing to invest in pilot programs, I highly recommend you experiment with some of the premium products out there as they can offer some very cool ways to help your students grow their language skills. It's my hope that the mostly free activities in this book work as a launchpad to more explorations.

The ISTE Standards

In this book, you will find references to the ISTE Standards for Students on every activity. The ISTE Standards are a framework that allow educators to ensure that the work they're doing creates "high-impact, sustainable, scalable and equitable learning experiences for all learners" (iste.org/standards).

Since this book is focused on student activities, the specific focuses applied to each activity fall under the category of ISTE Standards for Students. Aligning language learning skills with technology standards means that some standards got a lot more attention (I'm looking at you, 1.1.c, 1.3.d, and 1.6.d) and others got less (sorry, 1.5.d—I've still got love for you, just not here!).

As ISTE has recently implemented a new approach to the standards, with more frequent updates and iterations, the appendix to this book includes the standards as they stood at the time of writing. If you're interested in the ISTE Standards and want to make sure that the alignment is up-to-date, you're encouraged to review the Standards and perhaps even consider taking the self-paced course (edushare.ing/ISTEStandardsIntro) to learn how to utilize the standards for your own activities.

At the back of the book, you will find a full cross-referenced grid, showing which activities hit which standards.

About Saving Time

One thing edtech proponents always like to claim is that doing things with tech will save you time. This is not true. It's not false, but it's not true. Tech can save you time, but often you won't notice it because learning new tools, setting up assignments, etc., all take time in the beginning. If you only plan to do something once, you might in fact spend more time setting it up in an edtech environment than you would just doing it on the fly for your students in an analog situation. One example that comes to mind is that it's much faster to play audio tracks from your phone or desktop (or even a CD player) than it is to convert the same audio to video, upload it to YouTube, then embed the video on pages where students can access it. But remember, once you've gone through the setup once, you've already got your content ready to go the next time you need it. So if you use those same recordings for three classes a semester for the next five years, you might not feel that you're saving time up front, but I can guarantee you're saving time on the back end. Also, once you have things set up, students can access the materials you've created anytime that works for them. This gives them the chance to revisit content they might have struggled with in class, or review it before a quiz. When I was a student, the only thing I had access to was my textbooks, which did their best to weigh me down and give me scoliosis, and if I wanted supplemental materials I had to haul my butt to the library or the listening lab to check out audio samples in the form of cassette tapes, which I was then responsible for not losing. What a miserable process.

Edtech does save you time if you're consistent and thoughtful with it, but jumping from one tool to the next with no plan for recycling your work will defeat the purpose. Saving time, though, should not always be the goal. Consider whether the work you're putting in makes things more equitable for students; when you're using edtech thoughtfully, the answer is almost always yes. I don't know about you, but I'd rather lose a little time up front and make sure my students have the opportunity to succeed than be constantly frazzled with last-minute prep and end up sending students out the door with no further access to resources.

Finally, I'm reminded of Parkinson's Law, which states, "Work expands so as to fill the time available for its completion." In other words, you may end up saving time by using tech, but then reallocating that time to work that was previously left incomplete, or possibly you might end up stretching out the time of completion for work that previously didn't take much time at all. This isn't a criticism, just a cruel trick of human nature. However, if you are intentional about how your time is spent, you will certainly find you've made gains over time, even though it may not be immediately apparent.

The Not-So-Secret Secret

Throughout this book you'll see me encourage you to think of different ways to apply the activities to match your context. I regularly ask you to consider changing or even throwing away things that don't work for you. I slide in encouragement to add or revise to accommodate your students. To let the cat out of the bag, one major goal of this book is to encourage all of us as teachers to build our own creative muscles and try new things in our classes. My dream is that we all start finding new ways to build more of our own engaging activities for our students, and I hope that this book points you toward a path of experimentation and fun. Let the explorations begin!

LISTENING

To hear each other (the sound of different voices), to listen to one another, is an exercise in recognition.

— bell hooks

technology has opened the world to more opportunities for authentic listening than any time in history. With the rise of YouTube, podcasts, streaming internet radio, and more, people from all walks of life are sharing about every topic under the sun in their own, authentic voice.

Traditional listening activities in language learning are about the furthest thing from authentic listening you can get. Actors or teachers diligently went into studios to record slow, enunciated, and simplified versions of the language they taught to help scaffold the listening and make it more accessible to students. But as listening skills specialist Sheila Thorn points out, most scaffolded listening doesn't teach students how to listen, but instead checks their comprehension of language, grammar, etc. Today, though, capturing and having students work with authentic listening samples is easier than ever; we just need to work on keeping our teaching up with the tech!

There is, of course, a place for scaffolded listening, as is clear when we're working with beginners. The great thing about living in the modern world is that we all have the resources we need just a few clicks away: fully authentic audio from everyday people, natural-seeming dialogues from professional actors, and yes—even over-enunciated readings from well-meaning language teachers.

Keep an ear out for interesting audio and save it somewhere that you can access later. The world is becoming more and more audio-friendly, and with AI being so good at transcribing audio to text, we've never been in a more media-rich environment for language learners.

The activities in this section are only scratching the surface, and I hope they give you some inspiration to see what you come up with for your own listening activities.

JEOPARDISTINCTIONS

 *Students will enhance their listening skills by identifying minimal pair or matching sounds in a Jeopardy-style game.*

ISTE STANDARDS
1.1.c / 1.5.c / 1.7.b / 1.7.c

RESOURCES
brentgwarner.com/
jeopardistinctions

Introduction

Students who are just beginning their English learning journey often struggle to distinguish the difference between phonemes that native speakers take for granted. Linguist and celebrated English teacher Penny Ur's simple "Same or Different" activity is a classic way to compare minimal pairs, and we can update it with some fun tech and make a gamified Jeopardy-style activity.

After you've explained the sound you're focusing on and how to distinguish between the minimal pairs you're working on, launch the game for a fun and engaging way to practice and review.

Activity Outline

Setup

- Record audio of minimal pairs.
- Build the Jeopardy game. Note that the goal here is just to distinguish minimal pairs, so there's no need to build categories unless you want to expand on the game in your own way.
- Insert the audio into the game. Online, you can embed audio, while in PowerPoint you can put it into your slides directly.

Activity

- Introduce the Jeopardy game format to the students. For students familiar with the game, you may want to clarify that this version doesn't require giving their answer in the form of a question.
- Separate students into groups as you see fit.
- Have the first group select a category and point value, then everybody listens to the recorded sound clue. Groups need to discuss

their decision before answering, so be prepared for ambitious students who don't wait to raise their hand or shout out the answer.

- When groups are ready, their leader or all group members should raise their hand.
- Note that they are only listening for whether the sound is the same or different, so there is no opportunity for other groups to guess if the guessing group got it wrong.
- Give or take away points to each group depending on their answers.

Teacher's Role

- Put on your best Game Show Host persona.
- Facilitate the game, ensuring smooth progress and adherence to the rules.
- Help students review the sounds as they move through the game.
- Depending on your class, you may want to make rules like "no choosing from the 200-point rows until all of the 100-point questions have been answered."

Reflection

- After completing the game, have students discuss how often they agreed or disagreed with their groups.
- Have students share which words they're still struggling to hear the difference between.

Extensions

- If you're using an online game, share the link with students to visit and review on their own time.
- Share a list of the minimal pairs and encourage students to use an online dictionary to listen to the sounds at home.
- Record a combination of the minimal pair three times ("pat," "pat," "pet") and have students determine which, if any, sounds different from the others.

Materials/Tools

There are a lot of options out there for Jeopardy templates. Some are free and others cost a few dollars. As is usually the case, you get what you pay for. Here are the options I trust:

JeopardyLabs.com is a clean and easy way to make templates online. They're great because they're always available wherever you have online access. It's free to use and

LISTENING

play with, but you have to keep track of your bookmarks and whatever you make is public. For a very reasonable one-time fee, you can get a lifetime membership that lets you manage your templates and make your games private.

If you want to up the level a bit, high school teacher Ryan O'Donnell makes outstanding gameshow templates at CreativeEdtech.com, and they're priced for teacher's budgets. This is much fancier and filled with sound effects, so it's a great way to get students in the spirit of things. Having a real PowerPoint file rather than an online game also means you don't need to worry when the internet goes out!

Write or Draw Your Own Ideas

TRANSCRIPTION TRACKER

Enhance listening skills and accuracy in transcription through correcting AI-generated text of audio clips.

Introduction

As students become more advanced in their English, they can fine-tune their listening with generative AI, offering them a hands-on approach to improving their listening skills. By engaging with auto-transcribed audio clips, students are challenged to identify and correct errors, refining their understanding of the spoken language in a variety of accents and contexts. This activity not only enhances language skills but also familiarizes students with the practical uses and limitations of AI in language learning. It encourages critical thinking, attention to detail, and a deeper understanding of the nuances of spoken English, making it an invaluable addition to the English language classroom.

Activity Outline

Setup

- Prepare or select audio clips of varying difficulties and accents.
- Search podcasts, news reports, YouTube videos, etc. to find relevant and engaging content.
- Auto-transcribe the audio using an AI transcription tool.
- Consider whether you'd like to add errors into the transcription.
- Move the transcription into a digital document to distribute to students.
- Prepare links to the original audio for your students.

ISTE STANDARDS
1.1.a / 1.2.d / 1.4.b / 1.6.a / 1.6.d / 1.7.b

RESOURCES
brentgwarner.com/
transcriptiontracker

LISTENING

Activity

- Students open the document to interact with the transcript.

- In your LMS (or linked directly in the distributed document), students click the link to listen to the original audio clips while they read along with the auto-transcribed text.

- Using the "Comments" feature in the **word processor**, students identify and correct any discrepancies between the spoken word and the transcribed text.

- Students may need to listen to segments multiple times, focusing on intonation, pronunciation, and context to understand the speaker's intent.

- Students submit the corrected document through the LMS or your preferred method of collection.

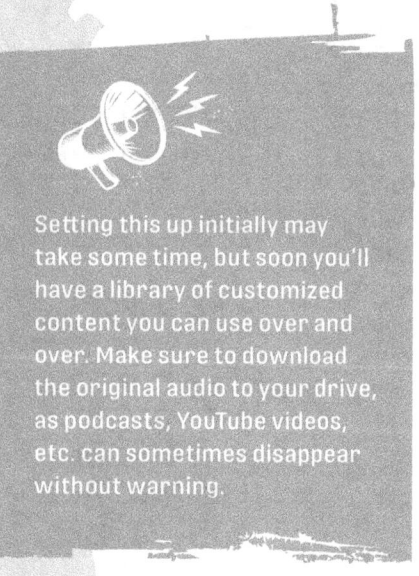

Setting this up initially may take some time, but soon you'll have a library of customized content you can use over and over. Make sure to download the original audio to your drive, as podcasts, YouTube videos, etc. can sometimes disappear without warning.

Teacher's Role

- Select appropriate audio clips that match the students' proficiency levels.

- Customize "errors" in the transcript to align with class objectives or unit language learning goals.

- Provide guidance on how to approach transcription corrections, including listening strategies and understanding common transcription errors.

- Facilitate discussions on the challenges faced during the activity and how to overcome them.

Reflection

- Students write a brief reflection on the process, explaining how many errors they found, and which they found the easiest and the hardest to correct.

Extensions

- Have students compare corrections with a classmate. Encourage them to listen to the segment again where there were discrepancies between their corrections.

- Students can transcribe short clips from their favorite English-language media or conduct and transcribe their own interviews, applying the skills learned.

- To start, keep these short (one minute or so), as it can take students a long time to transcribe, and they may lose motivation.

Materials/Tools

Before exploring the suggestions below, reach out to your campus leadership to ask about what resources your school has. Many schools will have access to some sort of transcription service to comply with accessibility needs. If you already have access to a service, start there!

If not, there are many auto-transcribers available, and they are all of different quality. Take the time to check the work yourself and see if you like the quality of the transcriptions. At the time of writing, many AI transcribers claim an accuracy of around 80%, which works well for this activity. However, AI moves fast and it may get to the point where it makes very few mistakes, so you may need to intentionally introduce mistakes into the transcript.

Riverside's transcription service (riverside.fm/transcription) is not exactly advertised front and center, but they do offer free transcription service with no logins needed! The output is pretty bare bones but should generally work well for the purposes of this activity.

Otter.ai does require you to log in, but you can get 300 minutes of transcription a month for free, which is plenty for the average teacher. The benefit to logging in is that it helps you keep track of your transcripts in a fairly easy to understand dashboard.

When you upload a video or audio to YouTube, it will automatically generate transcripts. If you already use YouTube to create content for your students, this could be a great choice.

PODCAST EXPLORER'S LOG

Enhance listening and comprehension skills through autonomous exploration and collaborative analysis of podcast episodes.

ISTE STANDARDS
1.1.a / 1.1.b / 1.3.d / 1.5.c /
1.6.a / 1.7.d

RESOURCES
brentgwarner.com/
podcastexplorerslog

Introduction

The Podcast Explorer's Log is a simple listening log activity designed to help students take advantage of the deep world of podcasts as a tool for enhancing language listening and comprehension abilities with authentic materials. In this activity, students exercise autonomy by selecting podcasts that not only match their interests but also their language comprehension levels. While listening to topics that they are specifically interested in, students will be exposed to a range of accents, dialects, and vernaculars, enriching their ability to understand various phonemes in English as well as building their comprehension skills. As the Podcast Explorer's Log emphasizes choice, it encourages learners to take charge of their learning process, increasing both engagement and motivation.

Listening to podcasts is a great homework assignment as it encourages students to build on their listening skills on a consistent basis but with content that is highly relevant to each of them. The entirety of the Podcast Explorer's Log can be done as a regular weekly assignment, or even more often, depending on the length of the episodes chosen by students. In the case where they choose longer podcasts, I often encourage them to focus on a 10–15-minute segment for the needs of the assignment, then continue listening on their own as they desire.

Activity Outline

Setup

- ○ Introduce students to the concept of podcasts and plant the seed that anybody with a smartphone or a computer can make one.

- Share examples of podcasts that may be interesting or level-appropriate for your class (see the online resources for a slide deck you can use).

- Guide students on how to use a **podcatcher** app to search for and subscribe to podcasts. Encourage them to find podcasts that pique their interest and are suitable for their comprehension level.

Activity

- Individually, students will listen to a podcast episode of their choice.

  - *Note:* Encourage students to read the descriptions of episodes and find something that catches their interest. I've found that it takes students some time to understand what it means when they are given the choice to listen to what they want. They've spent so long in school being told what to do, they often miss that they can really listen to whatever they like. I've had many conversations with students asking them why they chose to listen to something they weren't interested in, and they said it was because it was the first thing they found. Remember that you will need to re-emphasize over and over again that the choice, and thus how much they enjoy it, is completely in their hands!

- In groups, students will share their reflections, summarize the content, and analyze the episode's themes, language, and any cultural references.

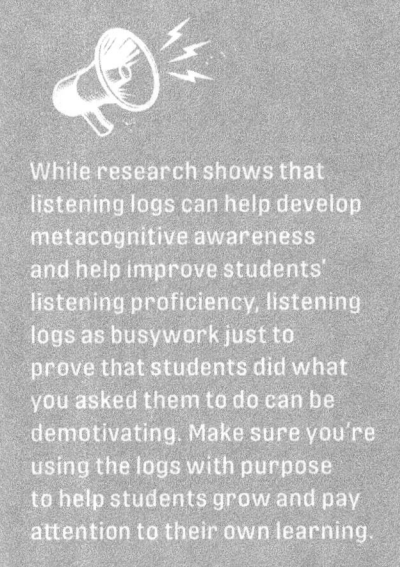

While research shows that listening logs can help develop metacognitive awareness and help improve students' listening proficiency, listening logs as busywork just to prove that students did what you asked them to do can be demotivating. Make sure you're using the logs with purpose to help students grow and pay attention to their own learning.

Teacher's Role

- The teacher will introduce podcatchers and guide students in selecting appropriate podcasts. During the activity, the teacher facilitates group discussions, ensuring every student participates and reflection is deep and analytical.

Reflection

- Students will maintain a listening log, documenting their thoughts, new vocabulary, and any questions or cultural insights.

Extensions

- Students can create their own podcast episodes on topics of interest or further research themes discussed in their chosen podcast episodes.

LISTENING

Materials/Tools

Whether you prefer students to use a school computer or their personal phones or other devices, there are tons of podcatchers available out there, so some exploration may be in order to find out what suits your needs. For many, PocketCasts.com offers a user-friendly interface for finding and managing podcast subscriptions. While known for music, Spotify.com also hosts a vast array of podcasts across different genres. If you prefer not to think about it, you can always use podcatchers included on most phones. Apple Podcasts (podcasts.apple.com) for iOS users and YouTube Music (music.youtube.com) for Android users are easy ways to get started.

Extra Space = Room to Explore

WHADDYAEER

Students will listen to reduced phrases and attempt to determine the meaning.

Introduction

When students start listening to English, they're often searching for distinctive sounds that they learned from professionally trained teachers or meticulously crafted audio files. The problem, they soon find, is that nobody actually talks in the ways they've been trained to listen. In *Integrating Authentic Listening into the Language Classroom,* Sheila Thorn's entire premise essentially boils down to the idea that students' struggles with listening come down to the fact that they're rarely ever trained to listen to authentic English. To help understand the differences between "textbook" English (and the accompanying recordings) and authentic English, many teachers start by getting into the fundamentals of reduction.

Whaddyaeer is a simple way to help students listen to the sounds in relatively distinct phonemes, developing an understanding of sounds that might be dropped or reduced.

ISTE STANDARDS
1.1.c / 1.2.d / 1.3.b / 1.5.c

RESOURCES
brentgwarner.com/
whaddyaeer

Activity Outline

Setup

- Record audio of reduced phrases
- Insert audio into Google Forms
  - Upload audio to Google Drive and then copy and paste the link directly into the Google Form, *or*
  - Make audio-only YouTube videos to embed, *or*
  - Use Mote to embed audio directly into the form
- Create "Short answer" text fields in Google Forms with the following categories:
  - What do you hear? (exact sounds)
  - What do you think it means? (the written English meaning)

- Under "Settings" activate the "Make this a quiz" option so students can see the feedback after they submit. Choose your preferred settings, and turn on "View results summary" under "Presentation."
  - On the "What do you hear?" question, click "Answer key"
    - Set points to "0" to focus on the learning and to show an understanding that what students hear is subjective and the spelling may vary depending on sounds they're used to in their **L1**.
    - Consider adding "There are no absolute correct answers, but check how close you are to the correct answer" under "Add answer feedback."
  - On the "What do you think it means?" question, click "Answer key"
    - If you're being precise or making a contest, you may choose to offer points for getting this right. Here you may choose to select "Mark all other answers incorrect" if you use the "Short answer" format.
    - If you're going for a more open activity, you can set the points to "0" and provide generalized feedback as above.

Activity

- Introduce the concept of reduced phrases to students. Sounds blend together in a way that is easily distinguished by native speakers but may cause serious problems for learners.
- Have students open the Google Form.
- Students listen to the audio and fill in the forms below each section.
  - As a class activity, you can project this and play the audio over classroom speakers as students fill in the information.
  - As an individual activity (or for home explorations) students can listen at their leisure and try to fill in the info.
- Students can check their answers and compare their responses to classmates'.

Teacher's Role

- If running this as an in-class activity, play the audio for the students and make sure everybody is on track with the right numbers.
- Review answers as a class.

Reflection

- Ask students to reflect on which phrases they still can't hear. Have them compare what they wrote down for the exact sounds versus the revealed meaning. Allow them to open up conversations on how the sounds they don't hear could be automatically interpreted by native speakers, perhaps because of context or grammatical structure.

Extensions

○ Create copies of the same forms but rearrange the audio. Students can try again for home explorations, moving more slowly. You may also consider making a version with slowed down versions of the audio.

○ Have students create dialogues where they use the reduced forms they're listening to. They can record or perform the dialogues, then have classmates try to identify where the matching phrases are being used.

○ Have students write down examples of reductions they hear outside of class, such as on social media, television shows, etc. They can bring the transcription of what they heard for classroom discussions.

Materials/Tools

Audio recordings: It's easy to record audio on your computer or phone with built-in software or easily downloadable apps. For my money, vocaroo.com continues to be the easiest way to make quick recordings online and download them for free with no sign-ins and no hassle.

Google Forms (forms.google.com) has a clean and simple interface that's easy to work with. For Whaddyaeer, you only need to paste a link to the recording, then add the two questions for "What do you hear?" and "What do you think it means?," respectively.

If you're looking for something that's a little more smoothly integrated, you can't beat Mote.com. You can skip all the separate recording and uploading, and students don't have to click out to listen to the audio. It's not free, but it's one of the few tools I unabashedly endorse paying for as it seamlessly allows audio to integrate into the digital experience.

Reductions are the first step to understanding the idea of an "acoustic blur," described by linguist Gillian Brown as sounds blending together into a mixed sound whose individual parts can't be distinguished, possibly because some parts aren't even uttered by native speakers in authentic speech. If you're looking to push the boundaries on helping students understand reductions, finding useful lists with common examples can be hard, though Penny Ur shares her own selected examples of collocations in *Teaching Listening Comprehension.*

LYRIC LOVER

 *Improve listening comprehension and interpretative skills through analyzing song lyrics.*

ISTE STANDARDS
1.1.b / 1.2.c / 1.3.a / 1.3.b / 1.5.c / 1.6.d

RESOURCES
brentgwarner.com/lyriclover

Introduction

While most of us probably consider ourselves music lovers at one level or another, we can all relate to the moment we finally tuned in to the lyrics of a favorite song and found ourselves doing a double take. Many of our students may be completely unaware of what their favorite songs are actually about, and Lyric Lover is a simple way to help them practice their listening skills while thinking more deeply about the words they're belting out in the shower. Beyond encouraging students to pick up the unique sounds of sung English, this activity can also support the development of a deeper cultural understanding of the world from the songwriter's perspective.

Activity Outline

Setup

○ Students select a song in English that they are interested in. The teacher provides guidelines for choosing songs (appropriate content, clarity of lyrics, etc.).

Activity

○ Students listen to the song, attempting to transcribe the lyrics, pausing as they listen.

○ After completing the song (or when the time is up), they search for official lyrics and copy them next to the lyrics they transcribed.

○ Students listen again, then compare and contrast, considering whether the official lyrics are more clearly decipherable this time around.

○ They discuss the differences between what they heard and the official lyrics with partners.

- *Note:* At the same time, students may be encouraged to note new vocabulary, phrases, and any potential cultural references or metaphors in the song.
- Students attempt to interpret the meaning of the song and rate their confidence in their interpretation.

Teacher's Role

- Facilitate the selection of songs.
- Provide guidance on how to analyze lyrics.
- Help students with vocabulary and interpretation.
- Optional: Create playlists of the class selections for everyone to listen to later.

Reflection

- Students can write a brief paragraph on what they learned about the English language and culture through the song, or how they understand the song differently than before.

If all music platforms are blocked in your school, this serves as a great homework assignment. After all, for most students, "Listen to a song" is a pretty great alternative to writing an essay!

- Students share what lyrics were easiest and most difficult to hear and understand without looking at the official lyrics. With classmates, discuss the differences between what they heard and what the actual lyrics were.

Extensions

- Students can translate the song's lyrics into their native language, then compare it against translations from the web, giving them an opportunity to explore nuances or interpretations of translations.
- This activity can be revisited endlessly with different songs, encouraging a broader exploration of the sounds of English as well as the culture displayed through music.
- If students are struggling with interpreting the lyrics, consider sending them to songtell.com, where students can get AI to share the meaning behind their favorite songs.

Materials/Tools

YouTube is a great choice for this activity as it's easily accessible (assuming your school isn't blocking it) and has most popular songs available, even if the artist didn't make a music video. Alternatively, any music streaming service available to you and your students works well.

While many streaming services offer lyrics, they don't always have them for every song. There are many websites, blogs, and wikis that allow people to share lyrics (and sometimes disagree, when musicians choose not to release "official" lyrics). Some of the most popular are Lyrics.com, Genius.com, and AZLyrics.com. Depending on how obscure your students' tastes are, if they can't find their song on one site, they may find more luck on another.

LyricsTraining.com is also an excellent choice for gamified listening. It's a free site built for language learners and teachers, and worth checking out as it can make a competition out of listening. I highly recommend checking it out and seeing how it fits your needs. My hesitation in using it as the base for Lyric Lover is that it can feel very high pressure, and even though there is a wide variety of genres represented, the selection of songs is limited and your students' favorite choices may not be available.

Finally, any word processor you have access to will help out for transcribing and interpreting.

Got Other Ideas? Write 'Em Here!

SKETCH & GUESS

A simple online version of the classic listening exercise.

Introduction

This activity, in which one student draws what another describes, is as old as the language learning classroom, but they say the classics never go out of style. This virtual version doesn't need much explanation, but it's worth paying attention to the potential for reflections and extensions that running this activity digitally can add to the activity. I recommend this version for fully online classes or as homework. If students are in a physical classroom together, having them draw on paper or a whiteboard is fail-safe and fast.

Activity Outline

Setup

- Arrange students into pairs.

- Provide students with different sets of pictures to work from or have them find a picture they like through image searches (I like Google's Quick, Draw!) or possibly even their own photo library.

  - Giving different links or images to some students while hiding it from others is surprisingly challenging to do digitally. I suggest creating breakout rooms just for sharing links in addition to breakout rooms that students will use when they do their work. First, have students go to breakout room A and B, respectively, where you can jump in and quickly share a link with all the people in each room at once, then have students move into their own breakout rooms for pair work.

- Ensure all participants are familiar with the digital drawing tool and screen recording software (if used).

ISTE STANDARDS
1.1.c / 1.2.b / 1.6.b / 1.6.d

RESOURCES
brentgwarner.com/
sketchandguess

LISTENING

Activity

- Student A describes an image or scene.

  - Booster challenge: Student A turns off their camera so Student B has to rely solely on their listening without nonverbal hints like watching Student A's mouth or checking body language.

- Student B draws on the digital whiteboard based on the description. When they are done, they will share the screen.

- After completion, roles are reversed: Student B describes, and Student A draws.

- Optionally, record the audio of the description for later review.

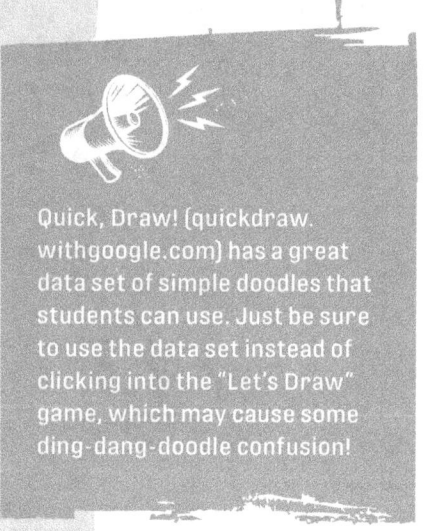

Quick, Draw! (quickdraw.withgoogle.com) has a great data set of simple doodles that students can use. Just be sure to use the data set instead of clicking into the "Let's Draw" game, which may cause some ding-dang-doodle confusion!

Teacher's Role

- Pair students and send them into breakout rooms.

- Provide a demonstration of the digital tools if necessary.

- Monitor breakout rooms to assist.

Reflection

- Students discuss the differences between their drawings and the picture that was being described. What was missing? What was captured well? What language might have helped to get a more accurate drawing?

Extensions

- If students recorded the session, have them listen to the recorded descriptions to complete the reflection above.

- Save the drawings for a homework assignment where classmates can access the drawings and attempt to describe what they think the drawings done by other groups represent.

- Collect the drawings into a slide deck to use as a prompting launchpad for story writing.

Materials/Tools

The easiest option for tools is the whiteboard built into whatever program you're already using for your class meetings. If you're on Zoom, it makes sense to use the integrated Zoom Whiteboard (edushare.ing/ZoomWhiteboard). Likewise, if your school uses Microsoft Teams (edushare.ing/MSTeams), it would be easiest to use Microsoft Whiteboard (edushare.ing/MSWhiteboard).

If you want something a little bit more robust or have particular reasons for moving outside of your online meeting ecosystem, FigJam (figma.com/figjam) has become a popular option amongst educators for its flexibility and collaborative nature. It's also free for teachers and students, so at the very least it's worth checking.

For those opting to record the sessions, most meeting software has an option to record breakout rooms, and again—keeping it simple is usually the best choice. There are plenty of other options out there for screen recording, including Loom.com. Many of these options give free premium features to teachers, but even if students don't get an upgrade, the basic free versions will often provide enough recording time for an activity like this.

Your Ideas Belong Here

ORDERLY LISTENING

Reinforce listening comprehension skills by sequencing story events as presented by a storyteller.

Introduction

Orderly Listening is another classic listening exercise merged with modern technology to create an engaging, interactive experience for your students. Being able to embed a video and manipulable elements like text boxes onto a single tool like Google Slides makes it easy for students to focus on their listening skills with minimal distractions. As students listen to an audio clip, they are challenged to reorder scrambled slides to match the sequence of events in the story. For beginning students, you might want to use keywords exactly as they are mentioned in the embedded story, but as students become more advanced, you may decide to use more synonyms and summaries to ensure that students understand what they're listening to. This method not only improves listening comprehension but also encourages critical thinking and expands vocabulary.

ISTE STANDARDS
1.1.d / 1.3.a / 1.3.b /
1.6.b / 1.6.c

RESOURCES
brentgwarner.com/
orderlylistening

Activity Outline

Setup

- Prepare a slide deck presentation with both a story (i.e., from YouTube) and key events from the story in text boxes, scrambled vertically out of order.

- Share the slide deck link with students, ensuring they all have access to their own copy.

Activity

- Students listen to the embedded recording carefully.

- As they listen, students reorder the elements in the slides to match the sequence of events described in the audio. Note that some audio may present events out of order. In these cases, decide if you want students to arrange elements based on how the storyteller presented the information, or how the events actually unfolded.

○ Students may listen to the recording multiple times to ensure accuracy.

Teacher's Role

○ Provide the recording and the scrambled events on the slide deck.

○ Guide students on how to use the slide deck if necessary.

○ Monitor progress, provide hints, or facilitate discussions as needed.

Reflection

○ Students write a brief summary of the story in their own words in a new slide at the end of the presentation or as a shared class document.

○ As a class, discuss the different sequences proposed and consolidate understanding of the narrative.

Extensions

○ Students can create their own stories in audio format and design their own slide deck presentation for their classmates to sequence.

○ As mentioned in the introduction, you can revisit the activity by using more advanced synonyms or summaries for students to decode while listening.

○ Choose longer recordings with longer or shorter gaps between presented story elements to keep students on their toes.

Materials/Tools

Orderly Listening can be completed on any computer or tablet, but prepare ahead to determine whether you need headsets, which would be appropriate if you've got students working in a 1:1 setting.

Google Slides (slides.google.com) are a great option here as it's easy to embed YouTube videos directly into a slide and the whole activity can be presented on a single slide (or two if you're including the reflection). You can also choose to upload your own audio directly into Google Drive (drive.google.com) as an alternative to having a YouTube video.

Alternatives include Microsoft PowerPoint (powerpoint.office.com) (I recommend sticking with the web-based version rather than sending files around), Canva.com, and more. As always, experiment with what works best for you and your students.

BEHIND THE CURTAINS

Students will infer and create narratives based on audio cues, enhancing listening comprehension and creative thinking.

ISTE STANDARDS
1.4.d / 1.5.c / 1.6.d / 1.7.c

RESOURCES
brentgwarner.com/
behindthecurtains

Introduction

Behind the Curtains transforms the classic exercise of interpreting television scenes with the sound turned off by flipping the script, students instead explore audio clips without visual context, challenging them to listen closely and infer the unfolding story. This approach not only sharpens listening skills but also grows your students' creativity as they imagine and articulate the scenarios being played out. By engaging with this activity, learners practice critical listening, a skill often forgotten as it can be overshadowed by its visual counterpart, but it's vital in language acquisition.

With a careful selection of clips, Behind the Curtains is not only fun and challenging, but it enhances students' ability to interpret auditory information in English and encourages them to use their imagination and linguistic skills to construct coherent, imaginative narratives. This is simple to understand, but remember to be forgiving as it's incredibly challenging to understand a second language with no visual cues.

Activity Outline

Setup

- Teachers select and prepare video clips that are rich in dialogue, sound effects, and ambient noises.
- Put students into pairs or small groups.

LISTENING

Activity

- ○ Prepare students to keep an ear out for contextual auditory clues including specific vocabulary, intonation, sound effects, and more.
- ○ Students listen to the audio clips without any visual context.
- ○ Students take notes on what they hear.
- ○ In groups, students discuss their interpretations and collaborate to create a scene description based on the audio.
- ○ Students present their narratives or scene descriptions to the class.
- ○ Finally, the actual video is revealed.

Teacher's Role

- ○ Facilitate the selection of audio clips.
- ○ Play the audio for the class without displaying the video. In a physical classroom, this could involve turning off the projector while playing audio over the speakers. In an online classroom, this would likely be the audio-only feature in the share screen settings of platforms like Zoom.
- ○ Guide the listening process and support the discussion and narrative creation phases.
- ○ You may also provide vocabulary or contextual clues if necessary.

Ensure the scene selected is appropriate for the classroom in terms of content and language level. The activity can be adjusted for difficulty by choosing clips with more or fewer contextual clues in the audio.

Reflection

- ○ Students compare and discuss the differences and similarities between their imagined scenario and the one shown.
- ○ This could be turned into a short writing assignment or a video submission via platforms like Padlet or via your LMS.

Extensions

- ○ Students can act out "their version" of the scene, applying a different context to the same dialogue. Discuss how it works and where there might be problems with clarity.
- ○ Ask students to send you clips they found interesting to use for future repetitions of the activity. This is doubly beneficial: First, it ensures that it's directly interesting and relevant to students. Second, it helps build you a catalog of clips that you can continue to use in the future.

LISTENING

Materials/Tools

We can once again rely on YouTube here as a relatively quick and easy way to search for movie or television scenes. Finding good scenes can be tricky sometimes, so make sure to keep a running log as you find them. You can also search for cold opens from television shows, great movie scenes, or playlists developed for actors to practice dialogues like the ones included in the online resources.

Before you start, determine if you plan to use the classroom speakers or if you need to prepare headsets for all of the students. You will also benefit from planning ahead if you want students using a word processor or paper and pencils for taking notes.

Your Turn—What Would You Add?

Speaking

All the great speakers were bad speakers at first.
— RALPH WALDO EMERSON

Whenever I ask students what skill they want to improve, they inevitably say "speaking"!

I love working with students on their speaking, but from my point of view, using tech in speech and conversation classes has always been one of the clunkiest edtech experiences. Whether it's too many students trying to record in a room with bad acoustics, or people being unable to find where their audio file saved to, there are always little fires to put out.

But still! The enthusiasm I see from students when they're able to communicate with teachers, classmates, and perhaps most importantly, native speakers in daily life makes the little frustrations of tech evaporate.

Every day, the tech for speaking is getting easier and easier. During the COVID lockdown, a lot of social media platforms started experimenting with chat forums. Phones now let you record your voice instead of typing out a text message. Anybody can launch a podcast from the digital device in their pocket. The list goes on.

As with all the activities, start simple and work your way up. If you're not sure how the tech works, you might also consider enrolling an "edtech buddy," who will play the role of your student and tell you what they struggle with in accessing apps and services.

There are a number of companies working on using AI to help evaluate speaking, so keep an eye out!

VOICE VIBE

Develop fluency and accuracy in using a specific grammar point through an impromptu response to a custom message.

ISTE STANDARDS
1.1.c / 1.4.d / 1.6.d

RESOURCES
brentgwarner.com/
voicevibe

Introduction

I've been using Voice Vibe with my students for at least 10 years, but when I present on it, teachers continue to be excited to see such a direct and applicable use for Google Voice—something that is technically not an edtech tool. By utilizing the free Google Voice service, this activity provides a real-world application for language learning, encouraging students to listen and respond to voice messages. Once you have a Google Voice phone number, all students can call in at the same time and leave messages. Setting a predefined time limit means they will have just enough time to call in, listen to a message, and leave their response, but not enough time to give each other hints or collaborate. Normally collaboration is great, but I've successfully used Voice Vibe for summative assessments with no problems. This approach not only bolsters students' listening comprehension and spoken fluency but also challenges students to use English without overthinking. The activity is predicated on the pedagogical benefits of authentic communication tasks, which research has shown to significantly improve language acquisition. By preparing students to respond to an unknown question by focusing on a specific grammar point, students can practice targeted language structures at the same time that they're thinking on their feet.

Activity Outline

Setup

- Set up a Google Voice account.
- Create a custom message focusing on the current grammar point.
- Brief students on the activity and the grammar focus.

Activity

- Students are sent outside the classroom to call the Google Voice number.
- They listen to the message and then leave a voice response, applying the grammar point in their reply.
- Remind students to start their response by giving their names. While you probably recognize most of your students' voices, it can sometimes be harder than you expect. This also ensures accountability for the student's answer.

Teacher's Role

- Prior to the activity, record the custom message and ensure that all students understand the grammar focus.
- After the activity, listen to the responses, providing feedback and/or discussing common errors in class.

Reflection

- As a class, listen to the original message together and discuss what some possible answers to the prompt might have been.
- Have students ask questions for clarification.

Consider privacy and consent—students' phone numbers will show up in your account, so ensure they are comfortable and informed about how their voice messages will be used for educational purposes only.

Extensions

- Since Google Voice transcribes the messages that come in, you can copy the transcription and send it along with a downloaded copy of their voice message.
- Google Voice gives students the ability to listen to their voice message as well as see how it was transcribed, so you can ask students to analyze their own speaking as well as their ability to complete the task as assigned.

Materials/Tools

To complete Voice Vibe, students need to have their own phones or devices capable of making phone calls. Consider creative options if you've got students who don't have their own phones.

Google Voice (voice.google.com) allows users to send and receive voice calls and messages. You can record and manage up to 10 different greetings in the settings, so switching on a prerecorded greeting as you start this activity is as easy as can be. I also appreciate the time-stamped messages, so if this is used as a summative assessment, you can easily ensure that messages were recorded during your testing time.

SPEAKING

As an alternative, a chat app like WhatsApp.com could be used for similar voice messaging activities, providing flexibility in how students can engage with the task.

This Space Is Yours—Use It Well.

OPINION QUEST

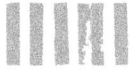 *Foster respectful debate and conversation skills through opinion sharing and polling.*

Introduction

Opinion Quest is an activity that is easy to do with no devices, but adding a tech layer such as Quizizz adds an element of surprise and community that can help engage less connected students. By committing to a decision on an opinion, then using English to support that decision, students have to think about their feelings on a topic as well as what language they can use to express those feelings. They also have to be willing to hold that opinion while challenging classmates to defend their own thinking, all while maintaining a polite interaction.

The gamified element will hold students lightly accountable to their original opinion, even as their thinking on a topic is challenged. The round will end with an understanding of how their opinion lines up (or doesn't!) with the rest of the class. This not only helps students sharpen their communication skills, but also allows them to be slightly uncomfortable when they potentially disagree with the crowd, but in a safe environment.

ISTE STANDARDS
1.3.b / 1.3.d / 1.4.d / 1.5.c / 1.6.d

RESOURCES
brentgwarner.com/ opinionquest

Activity Outline

Setup

- Review language used to disagree politely. This may have been covered in a previous lesson, or the focus of the day's lesson.

- The teacher prepares a quizzing or polling platform with a number of statements that can generate diverse opinions.

- Depending on your students' maturity level, you may keep this very light by asking about things like favorite ice cream flavors, or you may get more sophisticated in debating things like whether college should be free, and so on.

SPEAKING

Activity

- Students individually select their opinion via the poll.
- After voting, students find a partner with a differing view.
- Using provided sentence stems, partners engage in a polite debate to discuss their viewpoints.
- Once the debate concludes, the teacher reveals the poll results, sparking a class discussion on the diversity of opinions and how much they do or do not align with their classmates' opinions.
- Repeat with the next question and encourage students to find new partners.

A few intense debate topics:

- Hot dogs are/are not sandwiches
- French fries in milkshakes: for crazy people, or for the enlightened?
- Which is the best outerwear? Jean jackets/hoodies/windbreakers/other coats

Teacher's Role

- Prepare and monitor the online poll.
- Facilitate the matching of students with differing opinions.
- Guide the language use, highlighting respectful disagreement and the variety of class opinions.

Reflection

- Students record a brief reflection on what they learned from their partner's perspective and how their own viewpoint may have been challenged or reinforced.

Extensions

- If possible, students can do research to find larger opinion polls on the topic and where they stand in relation to the public as well as in relation to their classmates.
- Students can write short paragraphs incorporating the target language to describe the disagreements they had with their classmates and how the conversation ended.

Materials/Tools

There are a number of polling platforms, including Socrative.com and Mentimeter.com, but using the polling feature in a more gamified product like Quizizz.com may engage your students more and can offer more fun visuals and sound effects. Alternatives include classic systems like Kahoot.com, but remember to check and see whether the polling options are included in the free versions, as freemium options often rotate or become restricted over time. Most polling platforms work well on mobile devices or computers, just be sure to verify that each of your students has something to vote with.

For those adding the recording for reflection, Padlet.com, Screencastify Submit (edushare.ing/ScreencastifySubmit), or even your LMS are good places to get started.

Notes Go Here. So Do Aha Moments!

SPEAKING

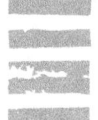

DE-SILENT FILMS

Foster creative storytelling and language skills by narrating dialogue-free animated films.

Introduction

For decades, Mr. Bean has been a standard in language classes because of the fun and engaging stories along with the fact that there is no speaking, which opens up opportunities for discussion and description amongst language learners. De-Silent Films takes advantage of the same concept but allows us to deal with a much larger selection of modern media, providing a unique canvas for ELLs to express their creativity while building their language skills. Using short animated films, students have an opportunity to refine their speaking or even to reshape the narrative. Because it uses an already powerfully developed visual medium, students of varying proficiencies can connect with the content and express themselves at their level. The activity is designed to enhance listening comprehension, encourage creative thinking, and develop speaking skills in a supportive, imaginative environment. It underscores the importance of student voice, offering a stage for learners to narrate their interpretations and stories, thus bridging language learning with cultural understanding and personal expression. Through De-Silent Films, teachers can transform passive video watching into an interactive, pedagogically rich exercise that captivates and educates.

Activity Outline

Setup

- Select a range of short, animated films with no dialogue. Prepare a viewing schedule and setup the classroom for an optimal viewing experience.

Activity

- Watch a short film as a class without any initial commentary.
- Split students into small groups or pairs and assign each a segment of the film to narrate.

ISTE STANDARDS
1.1.a / 1.1.d / 1.2.d / 1.4.a / 1.6.a / 1.6.d

RESOURCES
brentgwarner.com/ desilentfilms

SPEAKING

- Students draft scripts for their segments, focusing on narrative voice, vocabulary, and grammatical structures.
- Students use voice recording software to narrate their scripts.
- Optionally, combine audio recordings with the film clips using video editing software.

Teacher's Role

- Facilitate the selection of films, guide the scriptwriting process, provide technical support for recording and editing, and offer constructive feedback on language use and creativity.

Reflection

- Students present their narrated film segments to the class. Discuss the different storytelling approaches and language used.

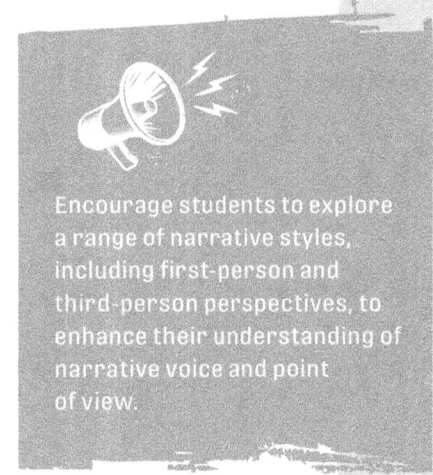

Encourage students to explore a range of narrative styles, including first-person and third-person perspectives, to enhance their understanding of narrative voice and point of view.

Extensions

- For advanced learners, incorporate the use of figurative language or specific grammatical structures. Revisit the activity with different films or even have students create their own silent animations.

Materials/Tools

YouTube serves as the primary source for dialogue-free animated films, offering a vast library for different themes and storytelling styles. Audacity (audacityteam.org) or GarageBand (edushare.ing/GarageBand) can be used for audio recording, allowing students to practice and perfect their narration before finalizing. Video editing software like iMovie (edushare.ing/iMovie) or WeVideo.com enables the combination of audio and video, providing a more immersive storytelling experience. Alternatives include using animation software for students to create their own silent films as an extension activity.

As always, make sure your projector or smartboard is working and ready to go.

FIBEROPTIC FISHBOWL FORUM

Enhance speaking skills through digital asynchronous discussions, incorporating specified language focuses.

ISTE STANDARDS
1.1.c / 1.1.d / 1.2.b / 1.3.b / 1.6.d / 1.7.b

RESOURCES
brentgwarner.com/ fiberopticfishbowlforum

Introduction

In the Fiberoptic Fishbowl Forum, video technology allows us to move the traditional classroom discussion over to an engaging, **asynchronous**, technology-enhanced speaking opportunity. Utilizing the video function of a platform like Padlet allows students to not only practice their speaking skills but also to critically listen and respond to their peers in a controlled, asynchronous environment.

While thinking on the fly is an important part of live classes (and students are challenged to do this in activities like Voice Vibe), many students may also benefit from time to prepare their thoughts and organize their language. Shifting the fishbowl activity from impromptu work to a planned speaking activity can give students the stability they desire as they become more comfortable with the language focus you're working on, as well as speaking for extended periods of time.

This activity encourages thoughtful dialogue, as students must consider their words carefully when recording videos, as well as ensuring they're able to speak clearly for predefined amounts of time. Zoomed out, fishbowl activities also allow teachers to identify interpersonal communication skills, and allow students to both participate in and evaluate conversations. By integrating a specific language focus, students have the opportunity to practice whatever language you're bringing into the class, making this activity a perfect blend of language learning and technology.

SPEAKING

Activity Outline

Setup

- ○ Create a Padlet wall and select several students as the initial *Fish* to start the conversation. Other students will play the role of *Observer*.

- ○ Create a discussion topic that students may have a wide variety of opinions on.

- ○ Determine the language focus the class is expected to incorporate into their recordings.

- ○ Determine appropriate speaking time expectations to match your class's abilities.

Activity

- ○ Day 1: Selected students (aka *Fish*) post their initial video responses to a prompt, incorporating the language focus.

- ○ Day 2: *Observers* watch the videos and post their responses to at least two *Fish* posts, using the video function.

- ○ Day 3: *Fish* consider and respond to at least two of the video responses provided in their column.

- ○ Day 4: *Observers* post a synthesis or summary of conversations they have not yet participated in, reflecting on deeper conversation and analyzing the big ideas.

Ensure that all students understand how to use the chosen platform's video function and consider accessibility options for students who might be hesitant to record themselves. Setting clear expectations for constructive feedback and respectful interaction is crucial.

To ensure a balance of responses, consider adding rules like, "If one student already has two responses and another has none, you are responsible to respond to the student with fewer responses."

Teacher's Role

- ○ Monitor the Padlet, provide feedback, and facilitate discussions by highlighting exemplary use of the language focus and encouraging deeper analysis.

Reflection

- ○ Reflection is built into the activity, but it may be useful to focus the Day 4 responses specifically on reflection. Consider having students comment on which ideas they thought were communicated most clearly, or for self-reflection, what they would like to change in their own recordings to get their ideas across more succinctly.

SPEAKING

Extensions

○ Future sessions can explore different language focuses, or the activity can be adapted for peer feedback sessions on presentations, storytelling, or debates.

Materials/Tools

Padlet.com is a versatile digital bulletin board that allows students to create and upload various media, including video posts, making it ideal for asynchronous discussions. Recent updates to Padlet make it an excellent choice for separating work into groups and isolating response types. In my sample Padlet provided in the resources, students are only given the option to respond with video or audio, ensuring that they're practicing their speaking with intention.

Alternatives include Screencastify Submit (edushare.ing/ScreencastifySubmit) for video responses, and VoiceThread.com, which allows multimedia comments on posts.

Think of Something Else? Jot It Down!

PODCAST PULSE

 *Create bite-size podcasts on trending topics to enhance fluency and digital literacy.*

Introduction

Podcasting has long been my favorite medium for helping English Language Learners customize their learning journey. While podcasting for the ESL classroom really deserves its own book, Podcast Pulse can help get us started by integrating the creation of two- to three-minute podcasts on trending topics, encouraging students to articulate their thoughts on familiar subjects. This activity not only incorporates a practical use of language around topics relevant to their own lives, it also nurtures students' confidence and fluency over time. The iterative nature of Podcast Pulse encourages sustained engagement, gradually building students' competencies in both the language focus you want students to practice and fluency in speaking.

Note that podcasting, while incredibly powerful, can be an intensive process. It requires critical thinking, organization, clear understanding of language, and some degree of confidence in speaking. Not only does it require these "soft skills," but most students will also be learning the technology to make it work at the same time. Remember that these skills build over time, and the first day of doing this in class may be chaotic and confusing. I regularly encourage students to take a deep breath with the understanding that they're making a full English language production from beginning to end, and nothing great is made with ease. After a few cycles of this activity, you will find that students start taking control of the process and helping each other out, creating the dream scenario: Students using English to teach complicated skill sets to other students in English, all without thinking about the fact that they're proactively building both life and language skills that can transfer to other uses across a lifetime.

ISTE STANDARDS
1.1.a / 1.2.d / 1.3.d / 1.6.a / 1.7.b

RESOURCES
brentgwarner.com/ podcastpulse

SPEAKING

Activity Outline

Setup

- Introduce the concept of podcasts to students and encourage them to find English language podcasts on topics they are interested in listening to. Consider starting with the Podcast Explorer's Log in the Listening section.

- Help students understand the structure of podcasts (intros, transition music, content, outros, etc.).

  - There are many different types of podcasts, but to start it's a good idea to keep things simple. As you become more involved, you may find yourself wanting to expand into all sorts of podcast types: interviews, panel discussions, radio dramas, the list goes on …

- I strongly recommend creating your own examples that align with your expected outcomes for your students' work.

  - *Bonus:* Creating your own samples gives you time to explore the recording tools and editing software so that you can guide students through the process with some experience and confidence under your belt.

Activity

- Students research their topics briefly to gather key ideas.

- Students outline their podcast episode, focusing on a clear introduction, main points, and a conclusion.

  - Language Focus: Students should include two to three examples of the language focus goals you are working on. Make sure they are clear on how they will use the intended grammar point, vocabulary, etc.

  - Careful: After many years of having students create podcasts, I've found that the biggest problem is how many of them rely heavily on over-scripting and then robotically reading the script. A few ways to reduce the robot reading voice include:

    - Requiring an outline that only has two to three words per section they want to record, giving them a hint but not a script.

    - Having students practice in rehearsal pairs. Each student practices what they're going to say with their notes open, then they switch to with their notes put away. Keep practicing until they can do it confidently with no notes.

- Students record their two- to three-minute podcast, practicing their script and focusing on clear articulation.

SPEAKING

- Encourage students to record in multiple short sections until they become more comfortable with speaking into a microphone. Alternately, if students stumble on their words, you can encourage them to pause, take a breath, and start speaking again while keeping the recording going. They can edit the mistakes out later.

- Optional: Students edit the audio, add bumper music and transitions, import pre-recorded audio, etc.

- Students publish the audio to be submitted.

Teacher's Role

- Assist in the initial setup of the accounts for podcast recording.

- Guide students in selecting appropriate topics and crafting their outlines.

- Provide feedback on language use, fluency, and podcast content.

Reflection

- Students can activate an AI transcription service and use it to analyze what the computer heard them say in comparison to what they intended to (or actually did) say.

- Ask students to download the transcript and highlight where they used the language focus and submit it to you along with the recording.

- Encourage students to listen to each other's podcasts not only as a language learning exercise but also to get a sense of what they could be doing to improve their own recordings. As a side bonus, listening to ideas and opinions helps to foster a sense of community and shared learning.

Publishing the podcasts out to the world is an important point of the process. It encourages students to recognize that their voice can be heard by anyone in the world, giving them motivation to submit something stronger than they might have if they knew it would only be heard by their teacher.

Some of my students have reported back years after finishing my class that they're still podcasting to keep up their language skills! If ever I could claim a long-term educational victory, that would be it!

Extensions

- Students can revisit their initial topics with deeper research or from different perspectives.

- Challenge students to try collaborative podcasts with classmates on shared interests or debates.

SPEAKING

○ Students can include goals for what they want to achieve with their next recording. This could be anything from including multiple language focuses you've worked on over the term, to speaking more clearly, to using more advanced vocabulary. In the following submission, ask them to report back on how they did, building a consecutive growth cycle through all recordings over the semester.

Materials/Tools

In addition to a computer or device for students to record on, you can boost the quality of their recordings if you can provide them with microphones. This may not be in everyone's budget, so don't worry if it works better to just use the built-in mics. You may also consider providing headphones so students can better focus while editing.

Podcastle.ai offers a comprehensive platform for recording and distributing podcasts, accessible to users at no cost. The free version allows students to create unlimited audio, editing, and hosting, along with limited access to other features, including built-in AI transcription. The free version should be more than enough for classroom needs.

For students with more advanced technical skills, Audacity (AudacityTeam.org) is a free, open-source choice with a wide variety of options for students on Mac, Windows, and Linux systems. GarageBand (edushare.ing/GarageBand) is also a great choice for Mac users. If all else fails and the goal is just to get a simple recording with no editing or publishing, Vocaroo.com has proven itself to be a reliable, no-frills option.

AI CHATTERBOX

Enhance conversational English skills through dynamic AI voice interactions.

Introduction

While the AI revolution has sparked a lot of conversations and innovations on ways to improve the language learning experience, perhaps nothing is more powerful than the fact that students can now have an endlessly patient tutor right in their pocket, available to speak at any time.

AI Chatterbox is an easy approach to enhancing language learners' conversational skills by leveraging the capabilities of artificial intelligence. Through engaging with AI voice features in platforms like ChatGPT or Microsoft Copilot, students encounter realistic and dynamic interactions, getting closer than ever to mimicking conversations in English with other people. Even living in an English-speaking country, many English language learners (ELLs) complain that they don't get opportunities to speak English, or (more realistically) that they lack the confidence to get into a conversation in the first place. AI's ability to simulate natural conversation not only boosts linguistic fluency but also cultural competence, as students navigate through various topics and scenarios and focus in on language features that are important to them. The practicality of AI Chatterbox lies in its adaptability to individual learning needs, allowing for personalized feedback and scaffolding. Plugging in a simple **prompt** and beginning the speaking process allows students to practice whenever and wherever they want.

Activity Outline

Setup

- Check your AI chatbot of choice and confirm that it has voice chat compatibility. Some have this only on mobile devices, others have them available on desktop browsers. This technology is always changing and becoming easier to access, so make sure you're aware of the features available on whatever system you use.

ISTE STANDARDS
1.1.a / 1.2.d / 1.4.a /
1.6.d / 1.7.c

RESOURCES
brentgwarner.com/
aichatterbox

SPEAKING

- Teach your students how to access and activate the voice feature.
- Typically, this is by clicking or tapping on the microphone option on the main screen.

Activity

- Provide students with the prompt below to cut and paste into their chatbot.

  - **Prompt:** Let's play a game where you ask me questions about my weekend, and I answer using the past tense. If I use the past tense correctly one time, you give me one point. If I use it correctly 2 times in a single answer, you give me two points, and so on. If I use the past tense incorrectly or fail to use the past tense, you will take away 1 point. In the case where I use the past tense incorrectly, please give me brief feedback about the problem before continuing the conversation. The goal is for me to get to 5 points total. In order to keep the conversation as natural as possible, you will use my answers to guide your follow-up questions. Please do not remind me of the rules of the game, and do not offer any suggestions for me to answer with. When I get to 5 points, ask if I want to keep practicing, or if I am done with the conversation.

- Students will listen to and respond to the bot, keeping their language focus in mind.
- When students get to five points, they may choose to continue with the conversation or end the activity.

Teacher's Role

- Monitor progress, offer technical and linguistic support.
- Keep an eye out for times when pronunciation issues may impede the chatbot from understanding a grammatically correct sentence.
- Remind students that like humans, AI won't necessarily understand everything they said. These are the moments to raise their hands and ask for support and clarification.

As always, you're encouraged to change and adjust prompts and activities to your own needs. Feel free to change parts of the prompt to customize the experience, or add/subtract rules or expectations to meet the needs of your students learning outcomes.

Reflection

- ○ At the end of the activity, have students ask the chatbot to give overall feedback on how they did and what they can do in the future to continue to improve.

    - **Prompt:** Can you give me feedback on my strengths and weaknesses?

Extensions

- ○ Students can be tasked with building their own prompts to gamify a conversation. Consider setting this challenge with no further examples than the prompt above and see what they come up with. Then put them in pairs or small groups and ask them to work on original prompts that make fun conversation games anyone in the class can use.

Materials/Tools

The AI chatbot world moves at breakneck speeds, so by the time this book goes to press things may have changed and options may vary. Major players like ChatGPT.com and Microsoft Copilot (copilot.microsoft.com) are likely to be more stable choices for a long time but keep an eye out for other choices as they become available.

Note that at the time of this writing, most verbal chatbots cleverly convert to and from text, so while the pronunciation of "read" as present tense vs. past tense may be clear to a human in a conversation, the chatbot may not recognize the change at all, assuming that the student got the verb tense right using the prompt above. In the grand scheme of things, small mistakes (and even big ones) get missed and skipped in the language learning process all the time, but it's something to be aware of and keep an eye out for.

If you have headphones available, providing them for privacy and focus may help your students as they get into their conversations.

DEB(AI)TE PRACTICE

Enhance advanced students' speaking skills through interactive, AI-powered conversations.

Introduction

This activity integrates advanced English language learning with cutting-edge technology, offering students a unique platform to refine their debate skills in a challenging but low-stakes activity. After the teacher has taught the fundamentals of debating, students can use this activity to simulate real-life debate scenarios, providing a safe environment to practice articulating arguments, thinking critically, and responding spontaneously. While in-class debates with classmates work well, integrating chatbots into practice rounds and for homework allows students to refine their skills and to get unpredictable and challenging responses, mirroring the complexities of real-world debates. By weaving in language focus goals like the use of compound or complex sentences, this activity can help enhance students' linguistic capabilities and develops their critical thinking. When students interact with AI rather than another human, they may find themselves under less pressure to perform well while they are still learning the skill of debating in a second language. Keep in mind that the focus is on practical engagement, where the AI serves as a bridge rather than a barrier to effective language learning and critical debate skills.

Activity Outline

Setup

- Check your AI chatbot of choice and confirm that it has voice chat compatibility. Some have this only on mobile devices, while others have them available on desktop browsers. This technology is always changing and becoming easier to access, so make sure you're aware of the features available on whatever system you use.

- Access the online resources section for this activity to get the prompt you and your students will need.

ISTE STANDARDS
1.1.a / 1.2.d / 1.4.a /
1.6.a / 1.6.d / 1.7.b

RESOURCES
brentgwarner.com/
debaitepractice

- Teach your students how to access and activate the voice feature.
  - Typically, this is by clicking or tapping on the microphone option on the main screen.
- Prepare a list of debate topics suitable for the students' level and interests.

Activity

- Students choose a debate topic from the list.
- Provide students with the prompt in the online resources to cut and paste into their chatbots.
- Students initiate a debate with the AI chatbot.
- The prompt provided will inform the student whether they are expected to take the affirmative or negative side of the debate.
- The debate should follow a structured format (e.g., opening statements, rebuttals, conclusions). As always, if you don't like this structure, you are encouraged to modify the prompt to suit your own style.
- The prompt in the online resources uses the following structure:
  - Round 1:
    - Pro side, opening statement
    - Con side, rebuttal and opening statement
  - Round 2:
    - Pro side, rebuttal and new arguments
    - Con side, rebuttal and new arguments
  - Round 3:
    - Con side, summary and final plea
    - Pro side, summary and final plea
  - Judgment: The chatbot will act as moderator and make a judgment on the arguments made.
  - Feedback: The chatbot will give feedback on the quality of the debate, how to improve in the future, and whether the student successfully or unsuccessfully used compound and complex sentences.
- If desired, students can send transcripts of the debate to the teacher for review.

Deb(AI)te Practice overlaps with AI Chatterbox in a lot of the setup, but here the goal is to work on much more advanced impromptu thinking and speaking skills. As you look at these two activities, start seeing how you can use various prompts to create your own innovative speaking activities for students.

While AI chatbots offer a unique opportunity for debate practice, it's important to remind students that the AI's responses may sometimes be unpredictable or not entirely accurate. This activity is designed to focus on the process of debate and the skills involved with speaking at a more academic level, rather than the accuracy of the AI's content.

SPEAKING

Teacher's Role

○ Introduce students to debates and the structure of debating.

○ Introduce (or review) compound and complex sentences.

○ Ensure the technology functions smoothly.

○ Facilitate discussions on the debate topics and the AI's responses.

Reflection

○ Students use the feedback provided by the chatbot to create a strategy for a more effective debate the next time around. This could be done as a video-recorded or written assignment.

Extensions

○ Students can try the debate again using the feedback provided to them.

○ Have students copy the transcript of their debate to a word document and analyze their own work in comparison to the analysis given to them by the AI.

○ Challenge students to change the debate topic to something they are passionate about and see how well they do debating it on both sides of the argument.

Materials/Tools

Deb(AI)te Practice primarily uses AI chatbot platforms like ChatGPT.com, which allows for real-time, interactive dialogue. These platforms enable users to engage in complex conversations, making them ideal for practicing debate skills. Review the Tools section of AI Chatterbox for considerations.

While not strictly necessary, this may be another activity where headphones, if available, can help students focus on their work.

ROLE PLAY ROULETTE

Enhance improvisational speaking skills in the target language through dynamic role-play scenarios.

Introduction

Role Play Roulette brings together the novelty of unpredictability with your own language learning objectives, offering a high-engagement opportunity to practice speaking. Using a digital wheel to randomize both student roles and role-play scenarios, students are not only hooked by the random nature of the activity, but also challenged to apply their speaking skills in diverse and spontaneous contexts. This activity is great for warm-ups or quick reviews, and once students are used to the concept you can break it out at a moment's notice, even when you just need a change of pace. Incorporating both planned and impromptu elements, it's designed to enhance linguistic flexibility, promote creativity, and foster a supportive atmosphere where students feel comfortable taking risks with their language use.

I like to make this a fun activity with a variety of roles from common jobs to internationally recognized characters in silly scenarios, like fighting over the last piece of pizza or being stuck in a haunted house together. This lowers the affective filter and puts everyone at ease, but you can easily swap it out for more serious roles and situations to meet your needs.

Activity Outline

Setup

- Teachers prepare two digital spinner wheels to project: one with a variety of roles represented by icons or emoji and another with a range of scenarios.

ISTE STANDARDS
1.1.c / 1.4.d / 1.5.c / 1.7.b

RESOURCES
brentgwarner.com/roleplayroulette

SPEAKING

Activity

- If necessary, review target language skills.
- Students are divided into pairs or small groups.
  - Use pairs if you're going to have students perform in front of the whole class. Use small groups of three if it's a whole class activity. Students A and B can role play, while Student C can keep track of the appropriate use of the target language.

- Each student spins the role wheel to determine their character.
  - If working in small groups, have students determine who is Student A, B, and C, then you will spin and assign the roles to each respective student.
- The teacher spins the scenario wheel that the students will have to act out.
- Students perform a short impromptu role-play based on their assigned roles and scenario, using the target language.
  - You may choose to set specific achievement goals, like the performers need to continue for three minutes without pausing, or each student needs to use the target language two times before the role-play scenario can end.

If your tech is unavailable for any reason, this is easy to convert to an analog activity. Just print out the icons and scenarios on pieces of paper and have students pull them out of a bag.

Adjust the complexity of the roles and scenarios according to the proficiency level of the students to ensure the activity remains both challenging and accessible.

Teacher's Role

- Monitor the activity, providing support with vocabulary or expressions as needed
- Spot-check for use of target language
- Ensure equal participation and feedback.

Reflection

- Students can record their role-plays for self-assessment or peer feedback. Consider having students privately vote on their favorite recording, then play the video during the following class for review.

Extensions

- Set longer time limits for the skits.
- Add a third or fourth person into the role-play.
- Incorporate more target language skills from earlier in the semester.

Materials/Tools

There are many ways to make a spinning wheel online. A quick search should come up with many choices, or if you want something that's not a spinning wheel you can also look for "random name picker" or other variations. WheelOfNames.com is an excellent choice as it is free, has lots of visual customizations, and allows you to insert not only text, but also images, including transparent **PNGs** and emoji into the wheel. Flippity.net is a good alternative that allows you to save everything to your own Google Drive (drive.google.com) and gives a lot of ways to present the roles. If you're a PowerPoint (powerpoint.office.com) fan, you can even search YouTube for tutorials on how to make your own spinner in PowerPoint, which will enable you to ensure nothing is lost to the web should there be a Wi-Fi outage.

Got a Better Example? Add it!

Reading

Think before you speak. Read before you think.

— FRAN LEBOWITZ

In my classes, I often have the pleasure of introducing students to the first novel they will read from beginning to end in English. While I typically go the no-tech approach to the book itself (students are often—rightly—incredibly proud of themselves and want to keep the book as a lifelong keepsake), I always find lots of ways to supplement their reading with useful tools and strategies that they can use anytime they're reading.

Helping students see that extensive reading is the gateway to success in their second language can shift the conversation from something they have to do, to something they get to do in your class.

Over the past several years we've seen the conversation make a major shift in what constitutes "worthwhile" reading. Traditionally, it would have been books from the canon, academic essays, and newspaper articles. Today, we see teachers encouraging students to understand texts through graphic novels, blogs, and even social media posts. There are lots of disagreements about whether the younger generations read less, or just differently, but from my perspective getting them reading in one medium is simply an opportunity to build a bridge to another medium.

Reading can be overwhelming for a lot of language learners, so showing them simple tricks like long pressing on a word on their phone to bring up definitions, dictations, and even translations can be a game changer for many of them.

Getting students in the habit of reading may be our greatest charge as teachers. The activities below should help you have a good time making it happen!

STORYBOARD SCENES

Students create a storyboard or comic to visualize and demonstrate their understanding of a scene from a book or short story.

Introduction

Visualizing scenes from reading materials can be a fun way for students to show they understood their reading, and there's a lot of interesting research around the value of visual literacy and how it can impact language learning. For younger learners, at least, there are promising studies that show that visual learning can increase achievement and make learning more engaging for language learners. In this activity, students will read a story or a scene, then transform what they saw in their mind's eye into a visual format by creating simple storyboards or comics. Creating a visual for a given scene not only reinforces their understanding of the text but also deepens their creativity and critical thinking. While this activity can easily be done on paper by having students draw out pictures on comic panels, the resources available online allow students to explore a much wider range of visual elements, up to and including AI-generated scenes that create far more detail than most of us can whip up on the fly.

Activity Outline

Setup

- Ensure students have read the assigned book or short story.
- Provide students with a brief tutorial on how to use the chosen comic or storyboard creator tool.

ISTE STANDARDS
1.1.b / 1.1.d / 1.2.b / 1.3.c / 1.6.a / 1.6.b / 1.6.d

RESOURCES
brentgwarner.com/ storyboardscenes

Activity

- Students select a key scene from their reading material. For students who need extra support, have them plan out the scene by writing a description in their own words first. Encourage them to consider important questions such as:
    - Who is in the scene?
    - Where is the setting?
    - Where are the characters or important elements in relation to one another?
- Using the online comic or storyboard creator, students design a visual representation of the selected scene. Remind students to keep the book open to the page(s) of the scene and to review it for details.
- Students should decide whether to include dialogue, narration, and supplemental visual elements to accurately depict the scene.
- Once completed, students will share their storyboards or comics with the class through a digital platform or classroom presentation.

One powerful way to get students' gears turning is to set up this activity by reading a scene from a popular book, then showing the graphic novel adaptation of the same scene. See the online resources for some curated suggestions.

Teacher's Role

- Guide students in selecting appropriate scenes.
- Assist students in navigating the comic or storyboard creation tools.
- Facilitate a class discussion to review and provide feedback on the completed storyboards or comics.

Reflection

- Have students write a brief reflection on why they chose their particular scene and how creating the visual representation helped them understand the text better.
- Encourage students to discuss what they learned from viewing their classmates' storyboards or comics.

Extensions

- Students can create additional storyboards or comics for different scenes or other books.

READING

○ If you're playing with AI image generation, you may consider encouraging students to have AI generate the scenes your students have in mind. This will also be a good opportunity for them to practice their descriptive language on top of displaying an understanding of the reading.

Materials/Tools

Everyone will need access to a preselected book or short story. For some, this may fit in with a thematic unit, while for others it might be a one-off reading. Explore to see what fits the needs of your class.

The free version of StoryboardThat.com has some binding limitations, but creative users can use it to make some amazing scenes. The platform allows users to highly customize a variety of characters in all sorts of settings. Older students may find the graphics not quite to their taste, but the flexibility is enough that many can overlook the simplistic graphics. Pixton.com may be a good option for slightly older students, but make sure you're aware of the pricing and whether it's something you want to invest in.

If you're looking for an option with more flexibility, Canva.com offers a number of storyboard templates to run with. A quick search for "Storyboard" in their templates section yields seemingly unlimited results, so you may find yourself stuck with too many choices rather than not enough. Note that the increased flexibility means students will be adding elements to make them work in the storyboard/comic, as opposed to the tools above, which are specifically made for this purpose. Where the purpose-made tools are like being given a box of crayons and a coloring book, using Canva is more like being let into a fully funded artist studio and just being told to "go for it."

DRAWN TO READING

 *Enhance comprehension and recall of a reading passage through visual representation using mind mapping and sketchnoting.*

Introduction

Language teachers spend a lot of time helping students understand readings by showing them how to skim and scan, highlight key words, and even understand structures of writing. While all of these are great, a lot of language teachers end up stopping there and skipping what might be one of the most powerful ways of taking notes on readings and lectures: sketchnoting! Sketchnoting and mind mapping are processes of converting a complicated chunk of information into an easy-to-understand personalized visual representation of the same idea(s).

Engaging students in reading activities using mind mapping or sketch-noting can significantly boost their comprehension and retention, especially when reading in a non-native language, as it allows students to become active learners. Drawn to Reading encourages students to visualize their thoughts and understanding by creating mind maps or sketchnotes, which helps break down complex texts into more digestible parts. By using images, lines, and keywords (even translations), students can connect ideas more effectively, leading to a deeper understanding and better recall of the reading material. While this works very well with paper and colored pens or pencils, some students shy away from trying because they feel they aren't "good" artists. Taking the activity online gives students the opportunity to import icons, photos, and other media to help them bring their notes to life.

Activity Outline

Setup

- Ensure each student has access to a digital device and the chosen mind mapping/sketchnoting tool.
- Provide students with the reading passage.

ISTE STANDARDS
1.1.a / 1.1.b / 1.1.d / 1.3.b / 1.3.d / 1.4.c / 1.6.b / 1.6.c

RESOURCES
brentgwarner.com/ drawntoreading

READING

- Introduce the concept of mind mapping and sketchnoting, showing examples as necessary.

Activity

- Students read through the passage once for general understanding.
- On the digital platform, students draw or visualize any concepts they thought were important or that they can remember.
  - Remind students to space their images out so they can select them and move them easily later.
  - If ideas are connected, encourage students to place them near each other. For example, if students read an article about healthy living, and one chapter was about exercising, and they remembered the examples of swimming and biking, they might choose to have a muscular arm to represent the big idea of "exercise" and then a picture of a swimmer and a bicycle underneath the arm.
- Begin a second read-through, this time encouraging students to pause and fill in the mind maps or sketchnotes with key points, ideas, and unfamiliar vocabulary.
  - Students can use images, symbols, and keywords (including translations) to represent their understanding of each section of the text.
- After completing their visual notes, students review their mind maps or sketch-notes, filling in any gaps and ensuring they understand the main ideas and details.

Teacher's Role

- Facilitate the introduction of mind mapping/sketchnoting, providing clear instructions and examples.
- Monitor progress during the activity, offering guidance and support as needed.

Reflection

- Students can pair up and explain their mind maps/sketchnotes to a partner, discussing any differences in understanding.
- In a class discussion, encourage students to share how the visual activity helped their comprehension and retention of the reading material.

Extensions

- As students become more comfortable with sketchnoting reading passages, challenge them to try it for lectures. If they're not quite ready, they can use short online videos and slow down the speed to practice.
- Use this method with different reading passages over time to build a visual reading journal.

Materials/Tools

Your reading passage should align with the needs of your teaching, but it's good to remember that the more abstract the reading, the more difficult it may be to create visual representations of the main ideas.

Note that some people swear by the need to "hand draw" on a touchscreen device, but not all students or campuses are equipped with this more expensive tech, so it's fine to work with what you've got!

The simplest way to get started with drawing for an activity like this is by using AutoDraw.com. The tool allows students to draw whatever they like, but if they don't like their own art, there's a tool built right in that will interpret their drawing and replace it with a high-quality icon. The platform is flexible and easy to use, and students can even make individual images in AutoDraw, download them, then upload them to a mind mapping option like the ones below.

Mind mapping may be a good choice to get started with this activity, as linking together words and simple pictures can build an easy idea of the concept without demanding too much of students right off the bat. In this case, there are a lot of options, but a simple one that's free for unlimited (public) mind maps is Coggle.com. This allows students to type in their ideas, upload basic images, and incorporate emoji as icons. Students can also work together on a shared document if you want to turn this into a collaborative exercise.

If you already know you want to dig a little deeper, Miro.com is a great choice and free for students and teachers. While Miro is a significantly more robust system (meaning a bigger learning curve), some of the useful features for sketchnoting include a built-in icon database, access to Google Images, and the choice to include stickers, emoji, and **GIFs**. Miro is also fully functional across platforms and has apps available for iOS and Android devices.

Start simple! Don't demand too much of students the first time around. This is a skill set that takes time to develop but can have a huge payoff as the skill can transfer to other classes and subjects in the future. Students will also see that they can build a better understanding of the language through visualization.

Mind mapping and sketchnoting are typically distinguished by a focus on hierarchy and organization, using words (mind mapping) or a focus on big concepts and ideas using images (sketchnoting). I prefer to bring both together, allowing students to take from the best of both worlds.

This activity is a simple digital version of what can become a whole approach to teaching for some teachers. Check out Nichole Carter's excellent *Sketchnoting in the Classroom* (iste.org/sketchnoting) to get an idea of how you can start building out more work in your own classroom.

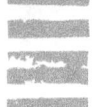

SOCIAL READIA

Students will collaboratively annotate a shared document, enhancing comprehension and critical reading skills.

ISTE STANDARDS
1.1.b / 1.1.c / 1.2.a /
1.2.b / 1.3.b / 1.3.d /
1.5.c / 1.6.c / 1.6.d

RESOURCES
brentgwarner.com/
socialreadia

Introduction

One of the biggest issues for teachers is getting students to do required readings before class begins. In the past, this used to be incredibly challenging; some research showed that as few as 20% of students completed reading assignments. But things are turning around these days as more and more teachers are turning reading into a social experience. Social Readia helps this process by treating the comments on a doc like a social media experience. The teacher can distribute the document to students, encouraging them to ask questions, share ideas, and respond thoughtfully to their classmates' comments. Setting specific guidelines for annotations helps to ensure a comprehensive and balanced discussion. This activity can be run for all different language levels, focusing on basic comprehension or summarizing main points and moving all the way up to developing counterarguments or adding novel ideas to the concepts presented in the reading.

Activity Outline

Setup

- Find and prepare the reading, making sure it's formatted for your chosen platform.

- Ensure all students have access to the shared document and understand how to use the commenting features.

- Assign the reading material and set clear guidelines for annotations (e.g., number of comments, distribution, key ideas, translations).

- Determine if you want the whole class to work on one shared document, or if you want to break them up into smaller teams. Note that 25 students working on the same document may seem like a lot, but the chaos can also build on students' motivation to keep it a bigger social experience. Depending on the size of your class, play around with how many people can work on one document successfully—you may be surprised!

Activity

- Students read the assigned document.

- They follow the instructions for annotating the document by adding comments.

  - Options for tasks on annotations are unlimited. They may be as simple as translating tricky vocabulary into their first language, or as complicated as inferring the author's intent by breaking down the text.

  - One trick to speed up the engagement is to require everybody on the document to ask at least one question about a specific part of the reading. Allowing them to choose what part will better ensure a large spread of questions across the reading.

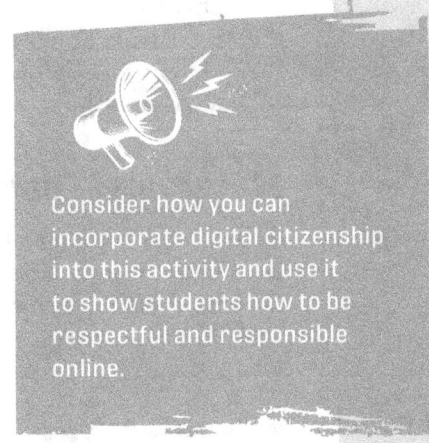

Consider how you can incorporate digital citizenship into this activity and use it to show students how to be respectful and responsible online.

- Students are expected to return to the document to respond thoughtfully to their classmates' comments and questions, doing their best to answer.

  - Encourage students to have fun here. They can provide links to videos that help, embed GIFs to keep things light, and even make jokes. Remember it's important that they enjoy the reading experience. The comprehension will come along with engaging with the text.

Teacher's Role

- Monitor the annotations and take note of any particularly interesting questions and responses from the students.

- Do your best to avoid commenting on the document directly yourself. Students will engage more when they feel that it's "their space." When the teacher comes in, the dynamics change, and it may become more important for students to feel like they're getting it "right" than that they're simply trying.

- After the assignment is done, project the document for the class and use it as a model to provide feedback on the quality and distribution of annotations as a guide for your expectations the next time around.

Reflection

○ Using the notes you took from students' comments, open up a classroom conversation during your next session together. Ask students to expand on their thoughts and find examples of students who responded well to their classmates, encouraging them to repeat their feedback for the class.

○ Ask students to discuss what kinds of annotations and comments helped them understand the reading better, then challenge them to try to incorporate similar comments the next time around.

Extensions

○ Students can export the document with comments to a PDF and then upload it to a chatbot. Have the students ask the chatbot to summarize the key challenges and takeaways about the article based on the comments left by students. They may also choose to interact with the chatbot to see what comments showed the best understanding of the reading, who asked the most engaging questions, and more.

Materials/Tools

Teachers have been using some variety of Social Readia since the first days of Google Docs (and for the hardcore explorers, even before that). These types of activities became even more common when Microsoft launched collaborative options in Word 365 and then through Teams. If you want an open-source option, Etherpad.org is worth a look.

While these features can be used in the platforms above, Perusall.com really stepped into this space with a dedicated service designed specifically for collaborative reading and annotation. If your goal is to get more reading done, Perusall created built-in features for tracking participation and engagement. They also have a thoughtful pricing model that lets you use it for free with suggestions on ways to pay if you find it useful.

If you think the majority of your documents will be PDFs, but you want something a little more multi-purpose than Perusall, Kami (kamiapp.com) may be the choice for you. The annotation feature allows students to click anywhere on the document, making it a little less messy than a word processor. The other features, even those in the free version, make Kami a good option for teachers who mostly just want to do what they've always done on paper, but now in a digital format.

TRENDING
TAKEAWAYS

Students will demonstrate reading comprehension by creating a social media video highlighting their top three takeaways from a chosen reading passage.

Introduction

Trending Takeaways is a fun way to move traditional summary activities or proof of comprehension assignments and bring the same skill set across to a medium that modern students connect with. By creating short, engaging videos summarizing their top three takeaways from a reading passage, students not only practice summarization and critical thinking but also develop their digital literacy and communication skills. Students can get as creative as they like. The activity is versatile, and even allows students to pick their own articles with ideas that are relevant to them or to classroom content, building autonomy and motivation. Keep in mind that if you're focused on content that is uninteresting or irrelevant to the students, they will quickly realize it's a lot more work to make a video than it is to simply write a list of takeaways. However, if you make sure the content matters to the students and they can start to see the connections to their own lives, they'll be ready and willing to spend far more time making sure they understand the original reading passage so they can share the ideas in a unique and engaging way.

Activity Outline

Setup

- Provide students with a reading passage that's relevant to your classwork, or allow them to select their own.
- Ensure students have access to a smartphone or computer with a camera.
- Introduce students to the social media video editing app they will use.

ISTE STANDARDS
1.1.c / 1.1.d / 1.2.a / 1.2.b / 1.3.b / 1.3.d / 1.6.a / 1.6.b / 1.6.c / 1.6.d / 1.7.a

RESOURCES
brentgwarner.com/ trendingtakeaways

READING

Activity

- Students read the passage thoroughly and identify and write down the top three takeaways from the passage.

  - Using their takeaways as the primary content, students plan the structure of the social media video, incorporating engaging elements like visuals, text overlays, and music.

  - They record the video, clearly explaining each takeaway.

  - Students edit the video to ensure it is concise and engaging.

  - They share the video on a class platform.

Over 50% of Gen Zers want to be influencers, and that number is only growing. Beyond a reading comprehension activity, this task also gives students insights into the kind of work and knowledge that might be involved in making even the simplest of online videos. If you want to dig deeper into the world of video production, it can be a lot of fun! Check out *Awesome Sauce* (iste.org/awesomesauce) by Josh Stock if you want some help incorporating video ideas into your teaching.

Teacher's Role

- Provide guidance on identifying key takeaways and structuring the video.

- Demonstrate how to use the video editing app. Many of your students will probably already be better at this than you. To make things more student-centered, you may consider identifying a few students who already make videos and have them show the class how to do simple videos.

- Offer feedback on the videos, focusing on comprehension and presentation skills.

- Encourage creativity and originality in the videos.

Reflection

- Students will watch each other's videos and provide constructive feedback. You may consider running a private poll to discover the class's top three videos and review them together. Discuss what made these videos strong and how they showed an understanding of the text. Sticking with the social media theme, you may rephrase this as: "Which three would you repost on your own social media?"

- Have a class discussion on the different takeaways and perspectives shared.

Extensions

- Repeat the activity with self-selected articles. This can be a particularly powerful way for students to take ownership of their own reading while staying on the same general topic with their classmates.

- If you're ambitious (and if you have permission), create a class social media channel to showcase the videos.

Materials/Tools

If your students have access to a phone or device with a camera and a built-in mic, the absolute best way to do this is to have students make videos in apps they're already familiar with and then download the video to their phone's photo album, rather than posting it on social media. While social media apps change in popularity, there's a good chance that whatever pops up from here on out will have the options to make and edit videos in-app. At the time of publishing, popular apps like TikTok, Instagram, and YouTube all have these features readily available in their phone-based apps.

Occasionally, you do run across students who either don't have social media or don't want to use social media services. On the simplest level, they can use the video recorder on any phone, or they can explore other video editing apps like Apple Clips (edushare.ing/AppleClips) or Adobe's Premiere Rush (edushare.ing/AdobeRush) available on both iPhones and Android devices.

CUSTOM
EXTENSIVE READERS

 *Students will create customized reading materials using AI chatbots, enhancing their reading skills with content tailored to their level and interests.*

ISTE STANDARDS
1.1.b / 1.1.d / 1.6.b

RESOURCES
brentgwarner.com/
customextensivereaders

Introduction

Extensive reading relies on the foundational principles that the reading material is easy for students and that there is a variety of material on a wide range of topics for students. Until very recently, this was a nice concept, but an impractical reality for many teachers. Over the span of years, we would spend countless hours either rewriting articles for our students or investing in a collection made by a company and then we kept our fingers crossed that it was interesting for our students. With the advent of AI, this is no longer the case, and teachers don't even have to be responsible for creating the materials anymore—we can hand it off to our students as a part of the process.

Building custom extensive readers with AI chatbots in the classroom can transform the way students approach reading. Extensive reading specifically steps away from many of the challenges of academic or intensive reading by focusing on materials that suit students' interests and proficiency levels. This activity takes advantage of AI to simplify complex texts or generate new, accessible content, putting the power into students' hands. While some students may not be used to this at first, by selecting topics of personal interest and ensuring the readability of the material, students can practice extensive reading more effectively, reinforcing vocabulary and improving overall fluency in a way that doesn't feel like traditional schoolwork.

Activity Outline

Setup

- Pre-teach the goals behind extensive reading, also called Sustained Silent Reading. Be sure that students understand it's for their pleasure, so they should really focus on their personal interests or hobbies.

  - Unfortunately, some students have had the idea of reading for fun drained out of them by school systems. Some teachers may find it useful to survey students about their favorite actors, athletes, hobbies, dream jobs, etc. before assigning this in order to give hints on topics they can read about.

- Have students select an article or topic they are interested in.

  - Remember that some students may come across an article that they would love to read, but feel overwhelmed once they get a few words in. These are the perfect kinds of readings for this activity, so encourage them to save these types of articles when they come across them, even if they can't read it in the moment.

- Make sure students have a sense of their reading level. When using chatbots, the more specific you can be the better, so telling it "I can read comfortably at a CEFR A2 level" or "My Flesch–Kincaid Grade Level is 5."

- Introduce students to the AI chatbot tools they will use.

Don't teach languages? This activity is a great way to get students on track with your subject by letting students read about it in ways that they're comfortable with. Encourage them to think of prompts for AI bots like "Write an article about how knowing geometry can help me build a better skateboard ramp," or "Create a paragraph explaining how the ideas in this psychology class can help me save money."

Activity

- Students will either upload an existing article to the AI chatbot for simplification or prompt the chatbot to create original content on a chosen topic.

- They will instruct the AI to tailor the text to their reading level, ensuring it is easy to understand. See the online resources for sample prompts.

- Students will read through the customized content silently and at their own pace.

Teacher's Role

- Guide students in selecting appropriate topics and using the AI tools effectively.

- Monitor the customization process to ensure the reading material is suitable for each student's level. Some students may not be aware that they're comfortable reading at a higher level than what they chose, so encourage them to explore.

- Remind students that if they're looking up too many vocabulary words or if they find themselves needing help to understand the content, they should lower the reading level.

Reflection

- Ask students to share how they felt about their reading. Did they find themselves focusing on the topic of the reading, or the reading process itself? If the latter, discuss what drew them out of the reading and back into the process. Have them share any ideas on how to mitigate the switch in the future.

Extensions

- Students can interact with the AI about the text. While it might be tempting to have students ask the chatbot to quiz them on the content, remember that the goal is not to have perfect comprehension, but to develop an appreciation for and love of reading. Instead, consider having them chat with the bot about the reading the same way they would do with a friend. They can build an interaction where they share their ideas and ask questions, and possibly even ask the chatbot to create follow-up readings.

Materials/Tools

Any chatbot that you have access to will be able to handle this activity with ease, even if students are using the free versions. ChatGPT.com, Copilot (copilot.microsoft.com), and Gemini (gemini.google.com) are fine choices, but there are many options available. Depending on the topics of reading, the need for accuracy of the bot may not be as important as it is in other academic assignments. As always, remind students that chatbots do have problems with accuracy, so even though the reading is for pleasure, students should also keep in mind that they may not be able to trust all the information they're given.

Note that some students may find a reading in a paper magazine or book, making it hard for them to upload to the chatbot. Don't worry! Most chatbots have a camera feature, so students can simply snap a picture of the paper and start by telling the bot to transcribe the text. Do be aware of copyright issues, as there are a lot of hot feelings and unclear laws around uploading text into these bots.

PARAGRAPH PUZZLE

Students reorder shuffled paragraphs to demonstrate comprehension and understanding of text structure and transitions.

Introduction

Reordering paragraphs in a reading passage is a well-used and still powerful activity that reinforces students' comprehension skills and their understanding of text structure. As long as I've been teaching, the classic activity of printing out a reading passage and cutting it into strips for students to place in order has been a great small group activity that gets students sharing ideas, analyzing texts, and reinforcing structural concepts we discussed in class. While a paper version still works perfectly well in an in-person class, doing a print version for homework or for online classes starts to create headaches for all involved.

Moving the activity online is easy and clean. You can still have students work in groups or individually. In some ways it can be better, as you don't need to spend time next to the printer cutting up dozens of strips of paper and keeping them organized between your fingers as you make sure you don't let any paper strips fall into the wrong group. As silly as it sounds, I've also had students look for where the scissor cuts line up as a way to find hints to the order. With an online version, you just pop your paragraphs into drag-and-drop elements and students can move each section around as needed.

Activity Outline

Setup

- Find or develop the essay/article you want students to read through and break it up into appropriate sections.

- Cut and paste the passages into each "strip" box on your interactive platform. Remember to keep the answer key readily available.

ISTE STANDARDS
1.1.d / 1.3.b / 1.4.d / 1.5.a

RESOURCES
brentgwarner.com/
paragraphpuzzle

READING

- Provide students with a link to the digital platform where the shuffled paragraphs are displayed.
- Review paragraph structure and transitional words/phrases as needed.

Activity

- Students read through the shuffled paragraphs individually or in pairs/small groups.
- Using the online platform, students drag and drop the paragraphs to reorder them correctly.
- If they're working in groups, encourage students to discuss their reasoning and use evidence from the text to justify their choices.

Teacher's Role

- Monitor student progress and provide guidance as needed.
- Facilitate discussions and encourage students to think critically about their choices.

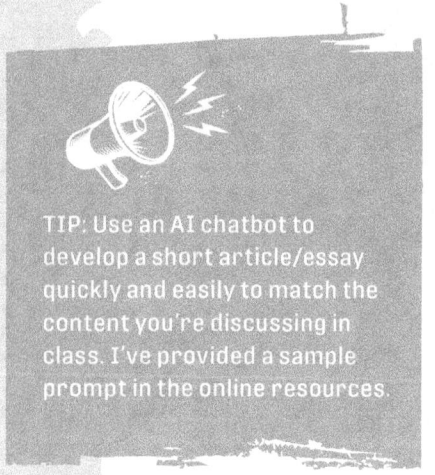

TIP: Use an AI chatbot to develop a short article/essay quickly and easily to match the content you're discussing in class. I've provided a sample prompt in the online resources.

Reflection

- Students share their reordered paragraphs and discuss any disagreements they may have.
- Open a class discussion on the organizational structure of the text and highlight any specific hints that provided insights into the correct order of the paragraphs.

Extensions

- Depending on the platform, have students annotate or highlight specific words or phrases that gave them clues as to where the paragraphs belong in relationship to one another.
- Consider throwing in distractors like off-topic paragraphs or repeated transitional phrases (using "third" in two different paragraphs explaining a sequence, for example). Tell students to keep an eye out for them. Or not, if you're feeling particularly rascally.
- For higher level students, you can leave one box blank and make students responsible to determine where it goes and what might be written in the box to make the entire composition appropriately coherent.

Materials/Tools

This can be done on any digital whiteboard, slide deck, or interactive platform that allows for manipulable elements. For many, Google Slides (slides.google.com) or PowerPoint (powerpoint.office.com) will be the best option because students are already familiar with the tools. For others who want a little more control, services like Genially.com or FigJam (figma.com/figjam) let you group and lock elements as needed so students don't accidentally dismantle the text boxes as they're moving pieces around.

Alternately, you could do a similar activity using an interactive polling tool like PollEverywhere.com, but be aware of character limits as you may need to break your paragraphs into smaller chunks.

Doodle Break Encouraged

CHARACTER CHAT

Students use AI chatbots to explore character development and motivations, enhancing comprehension and analytical skills.

ISTE STANDARDS
1.1.b / 1.1.c / 1.3.b / 1.3.c /
1.4.d / 1.6.d / 1.7.b

RESOURCES
brentgwarner.com/
characterchat

Introduction

As students become more advanced with their language skills and start reading novels, they may find they're missing out on details in the books or not understanding characters as well as they might. Using AI chatbots, students can now converse with any character from the book they are reading, allowing them to get insights into the character's background, thoughts, and motivations, and giving them an opportunity to have a greater understanding of and connection to the text. By comparing and contrasting the AI-generated responses with the actual book content, students develop critical thinking skills and enhance their ability to analyze and interpret literary elements. Character Chat allows students to make reading a novel an interactive experience unlike any learning activity we ever had before.

Activity Outline

Setup

- Ensure all students have access to a computer or tablet with internet access.

- Select a chatbot platform and create a prompt for the chatbot based on the book and your expectations for how it will interact with the students.

- Provide a brief tutorial on how to interact with the chatbot.

Activity

- Students choose (or are told to act as) a character from the book they are reading. The chatbot will act as another character in conversation.

- They enter your provided prompt to set up the chatbot for an appropriate interaction regarding the character. You may use the

READING

prompt below that I used in my class for Fahrenheit 451 as an example, or visit the online resources for more variations.

- **Prompt:** You will act in the role of Faber from the novel Fahrenheit 451. Your goal is to help the user gain a deeper understanding of the novel Fahrenheit 451 through simulated conversations with Faber. The user will take the role of Montag, and the user and the chatbot will have a discussion about the state of the world of Fahrenheit 451.

- Please maintain the following rules:

  - Chatbot will only speak as Faber and wait for Montag to respond.

  - If Montag talks about other characters from the book, remind him that you haven't met them and your insights would only be conjecture.

  - Do not give general information from the book that Faber wouldn't know.

- Students use the chatbot to ask questions about the character's background, thoughts, and motivations.

- Students take notes on the responses.

- Students may need to be constantly reminded to recognize the AI-generated nature of the information. Remind them that anything generated is not the intention of the author, but rather an opportunity for them to develop their own thoughts.

- They then compare and contrast these responses with the actual descriptions and actions of the character in the book. Encourage students to challenge any information they think is wrong or inaccurate. They can use these challenges as a part of their reflection.

Teacher's Role

- Guide students on how to formulate meaningful questions and conversation points for the chatbot.

- Monitor interactions to ensure students stay on task and provide support as needed.

- If necessary, facilitate a discussion on the validity and reliability of AI-generated content versus the book's text.

Note that if the book you are working with is well-known, the chatbot can do a VERY good job of impersonating the character, even matching the tone and style. In my *Fahrenheit 451* example, both the students and I found ourselves shocked about how well it captured Faber's voice, also leading to good conversations that helped them understand different aspects of reading literature.

It's important to continually reemphasize the importance of critical thinking and recognizing AI's limitations. It's easy for students to begin to think that the feedback being provided is somehow real or accurate. Remind them that while they may agree with the ideas, they need to separate them from the truth.

Reflection

- Students write a comparative analysis, highlighting similarities and differences and reflecting on any new insights gained.

- Students present their comparative analyses to the class or to partners.

- Discuss how the chatbot interactions influenced their understanding of the character.

- As a class, reflect on the benefits and limitations of using AI in literary analysis.

Extensions

- Encourage students to revisit the prompt, but to change the character. What would the conversation look like if they switched roles with the chatbot? What would happen if they decided to take on the role of the antagonist of the story, to see how they became that way? The possibilities are endless.

Materials/Tools

I recommend sampling this activity as you make decisions about your class readings. While most well-known content works well, you may find that chatbots have a harder time or create less impressive output for stories that are not as popular.

As with many of the other AI activities suggested throughout this book, the platform you choose for your chatbot is not particularly important. Consider what you have access to on campus, whether that's ChatGPT.com, Microsoft Copilot (copilot.microsoft.com), Claude.ai, or any of the other many large language models out there. I do recommend keeping an eye out for services that allow students to click a button to access a link to the chat, which can be used as a form of submission for the activity.

LONG READING SNOWBALL

Enable students to complete long-form readings in English by pacing their reading through recorded submissions.

Introduction

Long readings can be daunting for students, especially those who feel their reading skills aren't up to par. But if we encourage students to metaphorically "pack a snowball" by reading a small segment well in advance of requirements for the long reading, we can see that the snowball can turn into an avalanche of reading. When we break longer readings into manageable segments, we lower students' anxiety and boost their confidence in reading—a skill many students are highly self-critical about. If you have a longer weekly reading to complete a novel, you can get them started by having them record themselves reading an early segment of the reading out loud and submitting the recording.

In my own academic English classes, I've used this activity to great effect, and the students show an appreciation for an engaging way to get started with their weekly requirements. If the week's reading is due to be discussed in a Monday class, you might consider having the recording due on the previous Tuesday. A little psychology goes a long way, so if you have 40 pages of reading to do, consider having your students record themselves reading pages 4–6 of the week's assignment. This would put them at approximately 15% done with the reading on day one. On top of that, if you end the required verbal reading in the middle of a paragraph or passage, the students are likely to continue reading at least to finish with the current segment, rather than stopping mid-thought.

ISTE STANDARDS
1.1.a / 1.1.b / 1.1.c / 1.6.b / 1.6.d

RESOURCES
brentgwarner.com/longreadingsnowball

READING

Activity Outline

Setup

- Prepare a transcript of the two to three pages you expect students to read. Make sure students already have a copy of the book for themselves.

- Set up your chosen platform to make it clear to the students what you expect them to read and what specific pages/paragraphs of the book the passage can be found in.

  - I usually say something like "Start on page 46, fourth paragraph, starting with 'I was happy to see … ' and finish on page 49, second paragraph at ' … when the vehicle shuttered around the corner.'"

- Train students how to record themselves in the chosen platform.

- The first time you do this assignment, read the first page or so aloud for your students or consider playing the first segment from the audiobook if available. This models the tone and shows students how different the book can feel if they read it word-by-word vs if they treat reading it like a performance.

Activity

- The teacher assigns the week's long reading. Consider starting with a shorter long reading to start, then moving up as students build their reading muscles. You might begin with 20 pages and increase to 40 pages over the weeks.

- Clarify the due dates for each part of the assignment. For example, "Today is Monday, March 3. You have until Monday, March 10, to read this week's chapters. By tomorrow at 10 p.m., you need to have recorded the audio of pages 4, 5, and 6."

- Students begin the reading and record the assigned passage at home.

- If necessary, you can add in low-stakes check-in assignments to ensure students are moving along at an appropriate pace.

Teacher's Role

- Assess recordings and provide additional personalized feedback.

- You do not need to listen to all recordings of all students. Spot-checking works fine. If you're using a platform that provides automated feedback, build it into your assignment.

- Encourage students to have FUN with their recordings. If they're shy, remind them that the recording is only for them and for you. The more they get involved in the reading and put on an "actor's voice," the more they will enjoy the process in addition to building their English.

READING

Reflection

- Students discuss their understanding of the novel and self-assess on their ability to read the passage aloud.
- If you're using a tool that provides it, ask students to share their takeaways from the automated feedback on their reading accuracy and pronunciation.

Extensions

- If students become more comfortable with reading out loud, you may encourage them to form "book clubs" where they get together online to read segments and listen to each other.
- Play the official audiobook segment of the section that they recorded for themselves. Ask students to compare their readings to the official one. Be careful to remind them that you aren't asking them to be professional voice actors, but rather to think about things that they think they could do a little better the next time around.

Materials/Tools

If you use this as an activity to explore at home, you'll need to make sure that every student has their own copy of the reading. You will also need to find or make a transcript of the individual passages you want students to record.

While this assignment could be completed by having students upload a recording of themselves reading to a Google Form or through a recording platform like VoiceThread.com, I highly recommend looking at the Reading Progress Learning Accelerator (edushare.ing/MSLA) in Microsoft Teams (edushare.ing/MSTeams). The platform does have a bit of a learning curve for both the teacher and the students, but the payoff is huge, as it automates feedback for the students, checking the quality of their reading, their pronunciation, and their fluency in reading out loud.

This activity works most powerfully as a weekly assignment, so the first time may take a little more preparation. Once the students get the hang of it, they will be fine.

If students do the recording but struggle to get the rest of the reading done by the end of the week, consider breaking this activity down even further by having multiple shorter recordings due throughout the week.

EDTECH FOR MULTILINGUAL LEARNERS

Writing

I don't know what I think until I write it down.
— JOAN DIDION

Writing is one of the most challenging of all the skills in learning another language. It takes time, effort, analysis, and the willingness to be wrong. Not only that, when students move into academic writing, it's like they have to learn a whole new language again!

Still, writing can be one of the most powerful ways to gain mastery over a language, and for those willing to put in the effort, the payoff is immense.

In my mind, writing is where the world of technology and language learning first came together. Sure, we could listen to audio on a computer, read PDFs, or maybe even record our voices for short bursts, but writing was the one place where students could produce endless content—an open world adventure of language production that takes up next to no space and requires both no skill and every skill at once.

Most edtech companies that produce tools for writing stay focused on the tried and true: the basic word processor. Much like the mighty potato, the word processor sustains us, and very few people would deny its value. Also much like the mighty potato, we can add some spices here and there to perk it up when we need a bit more.

As you move forward, remember that writing is so personalized that it would be a shame for you not to adjust these activities to your classroom needs. Throw these potatoes in the food processor, add or subtract according to your needs, and cook them as long as you need. You're pretty much guaranteed something decent is going to be served!

MAKE A MEME

Encourage students to practice quick, concise, and impactful writing through the creation of their own memes.

Introduction

Memes have become a universal language of humor and commentary in the digital world. Make a Meme helps students develop creativity, critical thinking, and language skills by connecting a simple writing activity to a fun, digital form of expression that students are already familiar with. Students get to be both the audience and the creators, using popular meme formats to express their ideas, jokes, or perspectives. This activity not only makes writing fun but also teaches students the art of conveying messages succinctly and effectively. It's an exercise in brevity, wit, and creativity that doesn't require a ton of writing. Memes are engaging for language learning students and allow them to play with language, experiment with cultural references, and engage in a form of communication that's already a part of their way of seeing the world. Make a Meme works well as a low-stakes way to show students that writing can be fun and highly personalized.

ISTE STANDARDS
1.1.b / 1.1.d / 1.2.c /
1.6a / 1.6.b

RESOURCES
brentgwarner.com/
makeameme

Activity Outline

Setup

- Prepare any language points you want students to use in class.
  - Note that this activity can work well as a warm-up, so consider using your previous meeting's language points to revisit and practice here.
- Introduce students to popular memes and discuss the elements that make a meme engaging and effective.
  - See Materials below for a selection of classic memes, or create your own examples including more modern memes.

Activity

- Students select a meme from the template provided or create their own.

- Students write and add text to the meme, focusing on humor, relevance, or commentary. Students should be reminded to focus on the language point if this is part of your goal.

- Students get the link or download the image, then submit via the LMS, email, etc.

Teacher's Role

- Facilitate discussions around appropriate content and digital citizenship.

- Many students find challenges in expressing humor in their **L2**. Be patient and supportive as they make efforts here. Not everything will be laugh-out-loud funny, but if it's generally logical, they should be fine.

Reflection

- To build a reflection into a longer assignment, students can write an explanatory paragraph, clarifying what their meme meant and what background knowledge might be necessary to understand it fully. For example, some memes may require an understanding of certain athletes' personalities or the history of a long-running anime, which may not always be clear to others.

Extensions

- Upon completion, students can display their memes around the room (assuming a 1:1 classroom) and they can do a gallery walk, voting on their favorites.

- If you're not in a 1:1 classroom, consider having all students put their work on a shared document which you can then project.

Materials/Tools

There are a lot of websites that make it easy to build on popular memes without the need to create your own. Please be aware, however, that many of these sites share memes built by their users, and it's hard to know whether the memes that show up will be appropriate for your class. That said, a couple of the more popular sites include Imgflip.com and Kapwing.com.

Some teachers may prefer safer, student-friendly design tools like Adobe Express (express.adobe.com) or Canva.com. These are great choices and already have meme templates built in, but they are much less likely to have the specific images students see regularly on social media. Instead, there are thematically similar memes, but they're not the same. Think of them as the *Mac and Me* to your *E.T.* Still, they may be an easier option, especially if your school has subscriptions to these services.

SNAP 'N' SCRIBBLE

Build descriptive writing skills in English by creating social media posts with captions.

Introduction

On the surface, Snap 'n' Scribble can be pitched to your students as a fun, interactive way to blend social media engagement with English learning. Each week students are given a theme—maybe it's critiquing their favorite dish or narrating a weekend activity. The task? Snap a relevant photo and pair it with an English caption. But this isn't just frivolity dressed as education. It's a sneaky approach to developing English writing skills, albeit in a more contemporary format than traditional methods. Think of it as moving the old-fashioned diary-writing assignment into the modern world, where students can use a digital platform for sharing and observing the real world. When set as a weekly activity, students will build a sense of agency and become more consistent and creative.

More than just the language, however, activities like this can build communities of practice as students can be encouraged to work together to build a collective art project while interacting in authentic ways that are often lost in the artificial confines of the classroom.

Activity Outline

Setup

- Figure out your platform (see Tools below) and make your account before you ask students to do so.
- Determine a theme for each week. Ideally you would align it with other class unit themes, but you may choose random themes as well. Some possible ideas:
  - reviewing a meal
  - describing a weekend activity
  - sharing about an important person in your life
  - looking at something from a new perspective

ISTE STANDARDS
1.1.a / 1.2.b / 1.4.d / 1.6.b / 1.6.d / 1.7.a / 1.7.b

RESOURCES
brentgwarner.com/ snapnscribble

Activity

- Each week, students will capture a photo related to the weekly theme.

- Students should write a caption for the photo in English, focusing on descriptive language and personal expression.

  - You might choose to do the first post (or all of them!) as an in-class activity.

  - Determine whether you want students to write short and quick captions to get them going, longer captions as higher expectation assignments, or perhaps have them start the semester with two to three sentences and move into full paragraphs as the semester moves on.

- Post the photo and caption on the classroom social media platform or blog.

  - Reminder: Use caution and check your school's policies before posting anything publicly online.

Teacher's Role

- Introduce the weekly theme.

- Make sure your post is up before you announce it to the class. Your photo and caption should lead by example and give a general sense of the expected length of the post.

- Clarify any grammar or vocabulary expectations you will be looking for.

- Provide feedback on the students' writing and encourage peer comments and interactions.

Reflection

Students can reflect on their posts by discussing in class what they learned from others' captions and how they felt about the writing process.

Extensions

- Encourage students to comment on each other's posts to foster a sense of community.

- Revisit the activity by compiling the best posts into a digital yearbook (or if you can swing it, an actual printed one) at the end of the term.

Materials/Tools

You're going to need to make some decisions about what you're comfortable with and what your school requires for student privacy. We'll start with the original and broadest intention and scaffold down to more protected options:

Instagram: Real social media. Real easy. Of course, this is the least protected option, and you may have students that don't use Instagram or don't want to post school assignments on their otherwise perfectly curated accounts. If this is your path, I recommend having students make a "finsta" (fake Instagram account). They (and you!) can use the assigned school email account and only use it for these class assignments. Change all the settings to private, then have students start by following you. Once they've done that, they can all follow each other and you're off to the races!

Your LMS: Fake social media. Pretty easy. Your LMS is a good option for those with too many compliance loopholes to jump through. Students can simply upload the photo they'd like to share and use the accompanying text box to write about it. This will probably not feel as fun as a more customized platform, but it will get the job done.

Seesaw.com: Not social media. Dang easy. Seesaw is huge with those who teach young students, so this is a great option for K–6 teachers. Still, it's worth pointing out that teachers like pedagogical coach Greg Curran have done a lot of great work using it with adult ELLs. Regardless of age, this is one of the most locked-down platforms, but it's designed to be as easy as possible and locked behind a walled garden.

Can You Make It Better? Jot Your Changes

A ROSE BY ANY OTHER N(AI)M

Use a chatbot to generate collaborative poetic verses.

Introduction

Teachers have long loved bringing poetry into the language learning classroom. They're great ways to understand language, pronunciation, coherency, and culture. But not all students are comfortable when tasked with assignments to write poems. Luckily, AI excels here and can be a great collaborative partner, letting students play with language at a level that doesn't require them to think of themselves (yet!) as poets.

Activity Outline

Setup

○ Develop an introductory lesson on the power of poetry. You may wish to focus on free verse poetry, haikus, sonnets, or keep it broad and introduce a wide range of styles.

Activity

○ Students will choose a poetry form or style that inspires them. Use a variation of the following prompt to get started, depending on the type of poetry you want your students to pursue:

- **Prompt:** We are going to write a poem together. I will write the first line, and you will write the following line, making sure it rhymes and matches in pattern. As we write, you will confirm that each of our lines have thematic cohesion.

○ Have each student begin their own poem by writing the first line. This will be the seed for their creativity.

ISTE STANDARDS
1.2.c / 1.4.d / 1.6.b / 1.6.d

RESOURCES
brentgwarner.com/
arosebyanyothernaim

WRITING

- Have students check the chatbot's follow-up line and see if they like it.
- Incorporate the AI-generated text into your poem.
- Have students continue the process, alternating between their own lines and AI-generated ones, until they've completed their poem.
- Copy and paste the poem into a word processor and highlight the lines as follows:
  - Green = student-produced lines
  - Blue = chatbot-produced lines
  - Yellow = chatbot-produced lines that were edited and refined by the student.

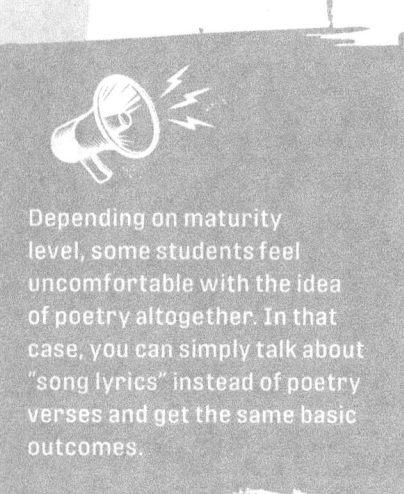

Depending on maturity level, some students feel uncomfortable with the idea of poetry altogether. In that case, you can simply talk about "song lyrics" instead of poetry verses and get the same basic outcomes.

- Have students submit when they are satisfied with the quality of the poem.
- You may find that the first time students complete this activity, it will be pretty clearly separated as green/blue/green/blue. With discussions and practice, students may find themselves returning to change words, revisit lines, and delete sections. The more time you're able to dedicate to practice, the more they are likely to find the motivation to customize the work so that it's truly theirs, and not "half" theirs.

Teacher's Role

- Provide guidance on poetry forms and structure.
- Challenge students to take different roles in the process. For example, you might have them adjust the prompt so the chatbot makes the first line and it's their job to find the rhyming line.
- Facilitate peer feedback and discussions on the poems created.

Reflection

- Have students discuss how much ownership they feel they have over the poem. Ask them to rank their perceived ownership in percentage (0% = not mine at all, 100% = completely mine). Their answers may surprise you!
- Discuss how AI suggestions influenced their poems and whether they would approach poetry differently without AI.

Extensions

- If students finish early, have them try a different poem style.

- Exploring Traditional Poetry: Compare AI-generated poems with poems from famous poets and analyze the differences.
- Poetry Slam: Organize a poetry slam where students perform their AI-assisted poems to an audience. To keep the AI theme going, challenge students to read poems better than an AI text-to-voice tool can do it.

Materials/Tools

This is not a big challenge for most **LLM** chatbots, so feel free to work with whatever you have access to. Some of the most popular current choices are ChatGPT.com, Microsoft Copilot (copilot.microsoft.com) and Google Gemini (gemini.google.com).

Notes, Sketches, Brain Dumps Welcome Here.

COLLABORESSAYS

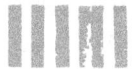 *Students will collaborate to create and refine an essay using an online word processor.*

ISTE STANDARDS
1.1.a / 1.1.b / 1.1.c / 1.3.b /
1.6.b / 1.6.d / 1.7.b / 1.7.c

RESOURCES
brentgwarner.com/
collaboressays

Introduction

Writing an essay is like making a pizza from scratch. It can be interesting, but it's way more fun to grab your friends and make one together. CollaborEssays takes the pizza party concept into the written world. It's like having a writing party online where everyone brings their best ingredients (words), and together, create an awesome essay pie. With widely available tech tools, students can work together in the classroom, or even at home from their kitchen. This simple activity will help students learn how to give kind, helpful tips to make their own and each other's writing shine, and they'll get insights into how others create their sentences, which they can then add to their own "recipe box." Let's fire up the ovens and see what students can make!

Activity Outline

Setup

- Ideally, this should not be the first time you have students writing on the word processor of choice. There's always a learning curve for less tech-savvy students, and it's better for them to be generally comfortable with creating and writing documents.

- Group students into pairs or small teams.

- One student should be the *Secretary,* the person who makes the document and shares it with their group member(s). The *Secretary* should also be responsible for submitting the essay. If students feel that this is an unbalanced workload, consider making roles for each group member, for example the *Secretary* as mentioned above; the *Grammar Guide,* who is responsible for making sure that grammar and spelling are accurate; and the *Researcher,* whose job is to make sure the information and facts presented are correct. Create or remove roles as necessary.

- **Important:** Make sure that students also share the document with you when they're sharing with their group members.

Activity

- Teams brainstorm and outline their essay structure collaboratively. I recommend a text-based outline structure such as MLA or APA to reinforce good organization and writing habits, but if you're working with younger or less academically inclined students, look at shared online whiteboards as an option.

- Once the outline is approved, have students begin the shared writing process. Each student should write in their own distinctive font color. I suggest purple, green, and blue, but any dark colors will do.

- Note that students almost always default to "I'll write the first paragraph, you write the second, and you write the third." This defeats the purpose of the CollaborEssay, so to avoid this consider the following techniques:

  - For the first 30 minutes of writing, only one screen can be open.

  - The person writing can only write what their group members are saying—no adding in their own ideas (yet).

  - After 10 minutes, the writer should rotate out and a new writer should start on a new paragraph.

- The goal here is not to finish quickly, it's to collaborate to make stronger work. Make sure to reinforce this idea regularly so students are relieved of the pressure of getting everything done on time.

- Team members review and edit each other's sections, focusing on constructive feedback.

  - Whether students continue working together in class or from home, they should make all feedback through the "Comments" tool that all collaborative word processors have. This leaves notes to the side of the document and lets students consider the suggestions before making them.

  - Paragraphs that were previously incomplete should be completed by a different team member. This will be clear to you because they will keep their color, so the point where the paragraph changes from green to purple (for example) is where the swap happened.

- Finally (and ideally back in class), the team should review the entire essay. You may consider asking them to leave all comments on the document as a way to see the collaborative work. It will be messy, but learning isn't clean!

Teacher's Role

- During the writing process, monitor the class to ensure they're writing collaboratively and not breaking up the assignment into separate parts. If you're doing this in person, the room should generally be loud.

- Once you've broken them of the habit of separating their work, log into their documents. (They may have already forgotten that they shared it with you on the first step, but now it becomes important!) Go in and make quick comments. If you're in person, you'll almost always see heads turn when they realize you're on their document at the same time.

  - I like to leave two grammar comments, two structure comments, and one or two content comments. This keeps them aware of what's going on without overwhelming them.

  - When they're working as a team, they can also spread the responsibility, so they feel less personally responsible for any mistakes.

  - My favorite part here is that when you jump between documents fairly quickly, students tend to be unsure if you're still "watching" them write. Students tend to up their game if they feel they're being watched. Just be careful to take the role of a supportive guide, and less of an authoritarian here.

- Take note of common issues throughout the writing and consider pausing the class for just-in-time remediation if several groups are struggling with the same issue.

Reflection

- You may consider asking students to write a private reflection outside of the group dynamic. Some students get frustrated with the group dynamic, but with a guided reflection they often see the value after the fact. Some guiding questions might be: "What are two things you learned from your classmates (either to do or not to do)?" or "What are two things you think your classmates learned from you?"

- Teams can share their essays with the class, discussing the evolution of their piece.

Extensions

- Groups can swap essays for peer review across the class. Keep the same groups together and have them collaborate on the feedback. Ensure that groups are giving kind and constructive feedback. While it's fine to spend some time trying to help classmates find errors, it's also useful to tell them what ideas worked well.

Materials/Tools

Most school districts either have access to Google Docs (docs.google.com) or Microsoft Word Online (microsoft.com/word), so this may be the key deciding factor in what you use. If you're opposed to the big tech companies, there are certainly other options to be found, but you may be sacrificing ease of use or useful functions that the Big Two have been fine-tuning for years.

NEWSROOM BLOGGERS

Help develop students' language and critical thinking skills by having them create individual news blog posts on topics of personal interest.

Introduction

Blogs were one of the first tools teachers started incorporating into their edtech-enhanced classrooms, and they still stand strong today. In this digital newsroom activity, each student becomes a journalist, exploring and reporting on topics they are passionate about. When writing is put out into the world, students often put more effort into their work. Depending on how deep you want to go, students can learn how to research facts, present balanced viewpoints, and write compelling news articles. Using the broad concept of a news blog allows for student flexibility and choice, allowing them to meet their own language learning needs while working on a collaborative classroom assignment. Students will learn to research, analyze, and present information in a journalistic style, building media literacy and critical thinking. This activity is robust and brimming with possibilities for expansion; consider whether this fits your class as a weeklong intensive activity (I wouldn't recommend it as a one-day activity), a full unit, or possibly even the thematic framework for the whole class.

ISTE STANDARDS
1.1.a / 1.1.c / 1.2.b / 1.2.d / 1.3.a / 1.3.b / 1.3.c / 1.3.d / 1.6.d / 1.7.b / 1.7.d

RESOURCES
brentgwarner.com/ newsroombloggers

Activity Outline

Setup

- Set up a class news blog on the blogging platform of your choice (see below).

- Discuss newspapers and websites as a class. You may consider pre-assigning a home learning assignment for students to find and share an article that is interesting to them as a way to get them exploring.

WRITING

○ Assign newsroom roles to each student. A basic setup would be to have every student be a *Reporter* and they write on their topic of interest to submit to you, the teacher, in the role of *Editor-in-Chief*. However, as things progress, you may prefer to have some students serve as *Sub-Editors* whose job it is to check the quality of work before it comes in to you as the teacher.

Activity

○ Have students brainstorm topics they'd like to report on. Topics can range from local events to global issues. They should be able to clarify why they want to report on that topic, and possibly how they will focus their reporting.

○ Students conduct research on their topic. Possibilities here vary widely:

- going to an event or place of interest for first-hand experience

- interviewing an expert on their topic

- watching a movie or TV show to review

- going to the library to research the history of a group, building, etc.

- etc., etc., etc.

○ Students write the news article in a word processor of choice. Make sure they incorporate whatever language point you are focusing on in class.

○ Conduct a peer-review session for feedback and fact-checking. If students are taking on the role of *Sub-Editor*, work with them to figure what they should be doing while others are writing. Perhaps they can take photographs that are relevant to their writers' stories. Maybe they can double-check that the information provided is accurate. Some teachers may prefer to have everyone take on both *Reporter* and *Sub-Editor* roles: students begin as Reporters, researching and writing for a specific length of time, then when everyone is done, they all become Sub-Editors and review each other's work.

○ Students log into the blogging platform and submit their work. Note that depending on the blogging platform and your preference settings, some blogs may be published immediately, and others may need to be approved. The options are all under your control and should be considered before you ask students to log into the blogging platform.

- Here you also have an option to expand your classroom lessons dramatically. Submitting work can be as easy as cutting and pasting the work in from their word processor, and if that's enough, great! But ...

- You can talk with students about design elements and how design elements are cultural and vary between different communities and countries, or even person to person.

WRITING

- You can encourage students to supplement their writing with visuals like photographs, drawings, or AI-generated images that help connect the ideas in the writing together.

- You can ask students to record a spoken version of their article to make it more accessible.

- And on and on and on. You get the idea.

Teacher's Role

- Assist in topic selection to ensure a diverse range of subjects and to make sure students are on the right path before they get started. Note that playing the role the Editor instead of being in the authority position as your students' teacher can soften the impact of rejection if you see problems early on.

- Cycle through students' writing. If you're using an online word processor, this is fast and easy. I like to leave notes quickly after they start writing—it may be daunting for some, but if you keep the notes supportive, they will think their writing is being checked the whole time and they'll be more careful from the beginning. See CollaborEssays for more.

- Facilitate the peer review process. Clarify your expectations on what you want them to look for in each other's reporting.

When dealing with the news, there are endless opportunities to push up the language level and the contextual learning. You can dive deep into ideas like readability, fake news, digital citizenship, and much more. The endless topics mean that students will always find things to write about that are of interest to them, regardless of the structural elements you're teaching.

Reflection

- In groups, students discuss what they were satisfied with about their writing and what they'd like to improve the next time.

- Have students consider different types of reporting they can do in the future, and what they can take from this round into the next round. For example, if students interviewed someone before, perhaps they can integrate quoting skills into a book review.

Extensions

- One common extension is to require students to respond to other posts from classmates. Use this as an opportunity to set expectations around constructive criticism and helpful feedback. Consider building sentence stems for lower-level students. Note that some students may respond to required responses poorly, so make sure you know your audience.

WRITING

Materials/Tools

There are many blogging tools available, and you should always check with your IT department as your school may already have something set up. I do not advocate for LMS message boards as an alternative, because students know they are in a closed environment, and part of the joy of a writing a newspaper is knowing people might read it! Edublogs.org is a top pick because it's specifically built for teachers and students, it's free, and the skills students will learn using it are transferrable to WordPress.org, which is still the primary blogging platform used worldwide.

Many teachers may prefer to start the drafting process in a traditional word processor like Microsoft Word or Google Docs. This can help students avoid accidentally publishing their work before it's ready. On the other hand, some teachers may prefer to incorporate online publishing—including its possible pitfalls—into the learning process.

Thought Of A Twist? Drop It In!

REVERSE ANALYSIS REVISION

Students will analyze an AI analysis of their work to see what revisions they should make to a paper.

Introduction

This is the very first AI assignment I asked my students to do, on the first day of class in January 2023, shortly after ChatGPT took the world by surprise. Students wrote a diagnostic essay, which I normally used to evaluate class and individual student needs to focus on over the course of the semester. This time, however, I let AI do round one. The goal was to show students what was happening with AI, and where its strengths and weaknesses were.

The crux of the task lies in the students' hands: They must critically assess the AI's feedback and challenge whether it's valid or applicable. This process encourages a deeper engagement with their own writing, building more critical thinking about their output. It's not just about accepting external feedback; it's about scrutinizing and questioning it, a vital skill in our new AI-driven world. This activity merges technology with critical thinking, emphasizing the practical skills of analysis and self-reflection in writing.

ISTE STANDARDS
1.1.a / 1.1.c / 1.3.b / 1.4.d

RESOURCES
brentgwarner.com/
reverseanalysisrevision

Activity Outline

Setup

- Students compose a diagnostic essay on a predetermined topic. Essays should be typed to make things easy for the teacher.

- The teacher copies and pastes the essay into the chatbot, prompting it to give feedback on whatever is relevant for their class. Below is a version of the prompt that I've used, but you may need to customize it for your own needs:

WRITING

- **Prompt:** Below I have included the prompt for an in-class essay. Next, I will submit a student's response to that prompt. Please clarify whether the writer shows a clear understanding of the original prompt. Please check the grammar and spelling. Then I'd like you to explain one or two strengths and weaknesses of their essay. Finally, give an overall evaluation of their writing. [ADD ESSAY PROMPT HERE]

- Cut and paste the response directly into the bottom of the student's essay and return it to them. Avoid any temptation to make adjustments to the feedback!

When I did this assignment, it immediately put my students on the back foot as to how willing they were to use AI. I found that since the more advanced students were able to critique the feedback a bit more, the students who might not have caught every detail became a bit more wary of it.

Be very careful about uploading student work to AI. Many bots train on uploaded data, so be sure whatever you are working with has student privacy options in place. Regardless, always be careful that you aren't uploading private, personally identifiable information.

Activity

- Once the students have the essay returned to them, clarify that you did not write any of the feedback, nor indeed did you even look at their essays. At this point, you have no sense of whether the feedback is accurate or even in the ballpark.

- Have your students read the feedback and comment on it using the word processor's comment feature.

  - You can be as specific as you like here. One approach may be to have students find one point that they disagreed with and one point that they can make sure to keep in future revisions.

- Ask students to write a broader reflection underneath the analysis including details about how they will update their essays.

- Have students rewrite their essay with their feedback and reflections in mind.

Teacher's Role

- The hardest part here is avoiding the temptation to look at the essays before students have done the first revision. I promise it will make your life easier, though. The quality of the second drafts will be significantly stronger, and that's before you've actually read anything.

- Open up the classroom discussion for reflection.

- Begin your normal feedback process, just one day later than normal.

Reflection

- As a class, have students scrutinize the AI feedback. Where did it get things right? Where did it get things wrong? Elicit feedback on categories it focused on.

- Discuss the reliability and limitations of AI in academic writing.

Extensions

- Students can later compare the revised essays with the initial AI feedback to gauge their progress.

Materials/Tools

Any chatbot should work. Some allow you to upload files, or you can simply cut and paste. Typical choices include ChatGPT.com, Microsoft Copilot (copilot.microsoft.com), and Google Gemini (gemini.google.com).

There are a number of tools for AI feedback that are popular with teachers, particularly because they're built for education. Look into BriskTeaching.com or MagicSchool.ai to see some options that can get you started.

Extend This Idea With Your Own Voice

AUTOMATED IDEATION

Use chatbots to break the "I don't know what to write about" roadblock that affects some students during freewrite activities.

ISTE STANDARDS
1.1.a / 1.1.b / 1.1.d / 1.3.a /
1.3.b / 1.3.c / 1.4.d

RESOURCES
brentgwarner.com/
automatedideation

Introduction

"I don't know what to write about."

"It's a freewrite assignment, write about whatever you want to write about!"

"But I don't have any ideas."

We've all been there. In fact, it's not the students' fault: We all struggle with work when we're not given any parameters. Part of the problem here is that many teachers are hoping to read something unique to break up the monotony at the same time as allowing students to explore their creativity. As teachers, we need to remember that creativity comes from constraints. Orson Welles is often cited as saying "the enemy of art is the absence of limitations." We might be hesitant to put the limitations on our students when we're asking them to be creative, but we can also hand that responsibility over to chatbots, better ensuring that the art will come. This activity helps introduce students to the very concept discussed above, then gives them strategies to use chatbots in order to overcome any writer's block.

Activity Outline

Setup

- Project a 10-minute countdown timer.

Activity

- Ask students to open a word processor or give them a piece of paper. When they're ready, focus their attention on the timer and tell them: "I want you all to write for the next 10 minutes. Ready ... go!" then immediately begin the timer.

- Expect to see looks of confusion, grimaces, shouts for clarification, etc. If you have the fortitude to deal with the uncomfortable moment, you can just point to the timer. After about a minute, you can let them off the hook and stop the timer.

- Ask around the room to find out what people do when they don't have ideas for a creative project. It doesn't have to be about writing; it could be about coming up with a new recipe, beating a level on a particularly hard game, or trying to make a viral video. Most of the suggestions will be a variation of getting inspiration from something that already exists in connection with something they're already interested in.

- Explain the value of constraints and how they help us to be more creative in our work.

- Introduce students to the idea that chatbots can create our constraints for us, then provide them with some of the prompts below:

  - **Broad Text Prompt:** I need to do a freewriting assignment but I don't have any ideas. What should I write about?

  - **Broad Image Prompt:** I need to write a journal entry for class. Can you generate a random image that can inspire some ideas for topics?

  - **Focused Text Prompt:** I need to write a blog post for a class assignment. Can you guide me through some questions to explore my interests, experiences, and curiosities, then use those responses to come up with some interesting topics to write about? Please ask the questions one at a time.

  - **Focused Image Prompt:** I'm interested in A, B, and C. Can you use those topics as a broad guide to create an image that might inspire me to write about a unique topic? Feel free to get creative and consider loose or abstract understandings of those topics.

- After giving students a few minutes to play with the generated text or images, put the timer back on the board. Repeat the line from before: "I want you all to write for the next 10 minutes. Ready ... go!"

- Students should be significantly more prepared, and you may find that they're unable to finish their writing in the time allotted.

WRITING

Teacher's Role

○ Help any students who feel like they're still not inspired by the AI-generated prompts. Encourage them to tell the chatbot that it's not generating what they're looking for, then to pivot to other types of writing. For example, they might have been getting too many prompts for creative writing when perhaps they would prefer writing a how-to guide.

Reflection

○ Ask students to discuss how they can use this strategy for future assignments.

○ In groups, have students consider variations on the prompts provided, or perhaps they can share completely new prompts that do a better job of eliciting topics to write about.

Extensions

○ Some students will do great work with less customized prompts. Encourage them to look at writing assistance tools like dailyprompt.com or storytoolz.com. There are many similar resources that can get students' ideas flowing, so encourage them to look around and find what they like.

Materials/Tools

Any chatbot should work, though some do not allow image generation depending on payment plans and other factors. Free choices that allow for both include Microsoft Copilot (copilot.microsoft.com) and Canva.com.

UNUSUAL PAIRINGS

Increase students' writing and research skills by having them write letters back and forth taking the role of interesting historical or cultural characters.

Introduction

This activity is designed to immerse students in the world of historical and culturally relevant figures through engaging online dialogues. Students pair up, each assuming the persona of a remarkable historical or cultural icon, then embark on an enlightening correspondence with one another. Through this unique interaction, students explore thought-provoking topics and witness how diverse perspectives can shape conversations.

Before launching Unusual Pairings, it may be wise to consider whether it's appropriate for students to represent themselves as certain characters. While it's fun and informative to role play, consider your choices carefully before asking students to begin their research. Alternately, instead of taking on the direct voices of others, you might consider having students take a step back from a first-person voice and instead report on their guesses about what that character might say. You could even provide them with sentence stems like: "I believe [person] would argue that [XYZ] because [evidence]".

Activity Outline

Setup

- Create a message board thread and split students into pairs.

- Each student is given a role. The only limit is your creativity. The options you provide to students could range from historical figures like Wangari Maathai, the first African woman to win the Nobel Peace Prize; to George Takei, author, activist, and online provocateur (Oh myyy!); to Mickey Mouse.

- Each pair is provided with a unique topic or scenario to base their dialogue on.

ISTE STANDARDS

1.1.a / 1.1.b / 1.1.d / 1.2.a / 1.3.a / 1.3.b / 1.3.c / 1.3.d / 1.6.a

RESOURCES

brentgwarner.com/ unusualpairings

WRITING

- Some pairings may be difficult to think of topics that both characters can discuss. One quick way to find a common area is to go to a chatbot. Try the following prompt: What's a topic that XX and YY could both talk about?

Activity

- Both students should be assigned to do research on what their character thinks about the focal topic. Ensure that students save the links to the resources as they should be included in their posts.

If the need to have students do research on a character's thoughts on a given topic is too much for the scope of your class, this could be simplified by having students take on the role of different characters from a shared novel writing to each other 10 years after the story ends.

For more student autonomy, you may prefer to have students choose their own characters. In this case, ask them to provide one historical and one modern character each. This will give you the freedom to ensure that the corresponding characters have enough variety to make things interesting. In this case, I recommend screening and approving their choices before sending them off to do research.

- Student A should be assigned to post first, sharing their opinions on the topic. The writing should include a number of questions that Character A might be interested to hear Character B's opinion on.

- Student B writes back, and the students develop the conversation by responding to each other's posts and answering each other's questions, advancing the storyline.

- Encourage the use of descriptive language, emotions, and character development.

- Emphasize the importance of respectful and engaging dialogue.

Teacher's Role

- Assign dates and times that you expect each student to post and respond by.

- Facilitate the activity by monitoring the thread, providing guidance, and ensuring that the dialogues remain on track.

- Offer feedback on students' writing style and online communication etiquette.

Reflection

- Students can write about whether they think the two characters could be friends in real life. Why or why not?

- Ask students to share whether discussing the topic from the perspective of their character changed or broadened their own thinking about the topic.

Extensions

- If you really want to have some fun, you could join in the conversation as a third character who challenges the ideas of Character A or B.

- Keep students in their roles, but have them rotate across different classmates to discuss other topics.

- Lead discussions on the transferability of online communication skills to real-life interactions.

Materials/Tools

This is easily set up on an LMS message board such as those provided by Canvas or Moodle, but the activity can be done anywhere that two students can contribute to a document. This could be as simple as having them write in a Google Doc (docs.google.com), or you could have them dive deeper into the world of digital tools and challenge students to find their own tool that they can work with to complete this activity. Allowing them to do this gives them not only the opportunity to practice language, but also to explore the Creative Communicator ISTE standards (iste.org/standards/students).

Add Your Spin. Literally, if You Doodle

EDTECH FOR MULTILINGUAL LEARNERS

Vocabulary

The difference between the almost right word and the right word is really a large matter—'tis the difference between the lightning-bug and the lightning.

— MARK TWAIN

by some counts you need about 10,000 words in a second language to become fluent. That can feel like a huge undertaking, but we should always remind students that language learning is a marathon, not a sprint. In fact, native speakers have lots of words that they don't know, too. Remind students that we're all on a lifelong journey of learning new and interesting words, and before they know it, they'll be able to look back at how far they've come with wonder.

Vocabulary acquisition is one of those things that seems so obvious on the surface, but the deeper you dive, the more you learn that teaching and learning it requires real dedication and thoughtful approaches. Luckily, technology lends itself beautifully to improving our lexicon, and it's only a matter of building habits to reinforce the learning of new words.

Language learners have two sets of vocabulary words—active and passive. The active words are the ones that are readily available to use without slowing down. The passive words are the ones that learners can understand when reading or hearing them, but struggle to pull out when needed.

As the word "passive" implies, students can't just sit back and let the vocabulary happen to them; they have to go get it! The activities below aim to engage the learner with vocabulary, helping to move more words to the active set.

SYNONYM SEARCHER

Students enhance their vocabulary by building a story using interconnected words from a thesaurus.

ISTE STANDARDS
1.1.b / 1.3.b / 1.3.c /
1.5.b / 1.6.d

RESOURCES
brentgwarner.com/
synonymsearcher

Introduction

This activity encourages students to expand their vocabulary and improve their writing skills by exploring the interconnected nature of words. While some research suggests that learning synonyms together is more difficult than learning unrelated words, language acquisition researcher Dr. Stuart Webb challenges this idea and proposes that learning synonyms for known words is a common and intuitive experience. In Synonym Searcher, we have some fun and explore the possibilities of adding to students' lexicon by threading synonyms together and creating a cohesive thematic composition. As they write, students incorporate new words linked to their original word, tracking their usage throughout the story. This activity pushes their ability to use synonyms naturally and also stimulates their creativity by challenging them to maintain coherence or explore thematic shifts. While the core goal here is for students to build their vocabulary, this activity also serves as an opportunity for teachers to help students develop their own particular writing styles that can align with the class outcomes. Keep an eye out for how the writing aspect of Synonym Searcher can align with your classroom curriculum.

Activity Outline

Setup

- If necessary, explain how to use a thesaurus. This may already be a part of your students' routine, or they may need explicit instruction.

- Determine whether students will work with a provided vocabulary list or if they will explore using words that are interesting to them. If students will choose for themselves, prepare them during a prior class session to keep track of interesting or useful words that they already know and would like to know more about, so they have a starting point.

VOCABULARY

Activity

- Students choose an initial word to start their story, either from the class list or from their own. This will be their key word.

- Students will incorporate the key word into the topic sentence of a paragraph.

  - Note that the writing style of the paragraph is endlessly flexible, so you might choose to align it with other lessons in your class, or you might choose a writing style you want students to work on: personal essays, restaurant reviews, flash fiction, etc.

- After they have used the key word, they will use the thesaurus to find other words with a similar meaning. Their job is to then insert the new vocabulary word into a logical place in their paragraph and continue moving forward.

  - Warn students that their work might feel forced if they try to put each word too close to the previous word. The goal is not to write as short a paragraph as possible, but instead to explore how words can connect to each other.

- During the writing process, students should track each word used. Highlight each word as it is incorporated into the paragraph and keep a running list at the bottom.

- Students are finished when they have included a minimum of eight connections and wrapped up their paragraph in a logical and coherent way.

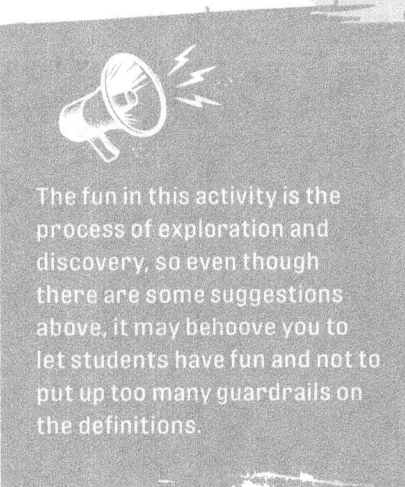

The fun in this activity is the process of exploration and discovery, so even though there are some suggestions above, it may behoove you to let students have fun and not to put up too many guardrails on the definitions.

Teacher's Role

- Introduce the activity and provide examples.

- Guide students in using the thesaurus effectively.

- Monitor the class as they are writing. Ensure that students understand the changing nuance between words. For example, on thesaurus.com, "espresso" shows up as a synonym for "coffee." If your student is doing creative writing about their morning routine, it may be fine, but any coffee nerd will tell you they are not the same thing, and the distinction is important. If a student is writing a how-to on making a pour-over and they start using "espresso" to describe the process, they will be far enough off base that intervention would be appropriate.

Reflection

- Students share their paragraphs with peers or the class.

- As they listen to their classmates read their writing sample, have them try to guess which words were the connectors in the thesaurus.

- Have the reader confirm the guesses of their classmates and clarify the distinctions between the words as they move down the list of words.

Extensions

- For more advanced students, challenge them to see how far away they can move from the original word by the end of their writing. For example, I was able to get from "coffee" to "parody" in eight connections (Coffee> Brew > Liquor > Spirits > Mood > Humor > Farce > Parody), but it would take some understanding of the multiple definitions of words like "brew" and "spirits" to understand how I got there.

- Alternately, if you find students are moving too far off path, challenge them to try again where the theme of the writing must stay connected to the key word the whole time.

Materials/Tools

Any dictionary or online thesaurus will do; just make sure that it's easy and intuitive for students to move through from one word to the next. Thesaurus.com and WordHippo.com are great choices that are easy to get started with. Still, if you want to have some visual fun, explore Visuwords.com for an online graphic dictionary and thesaurus that helps visualize word connections. Each node on the platform shows the connection between different words, and double clicking on a node then opens it up for more connections. It can be a lot of fun, but keep in mind that beginning and intermediate students may find they still need a language-learner's dictionary to follow along with all the words that pop up.

Students can do their actual writing on any word processor, making it easy for them to share their final work with you on your LMS or however you collect assignments. Some teachers may encourage students to write their submissions with good old paper and pencil, helping to bridge the analog and the digital. While it's not as clean as a digital submission, I do like this option as I find that some students do a better job of focusing when they aren't constantly fidgeting with switching between apps and web pages.

IDIOMAGINATIVE EXPLORATIONS

Students use AI tools to build visual representations of idiomatic expressions.

Introduction

While idioms can be a lot of fun, they can also be challenging for language learners, as their meanings are not always directly related to the words used. "What," students fairly ask, "does spilling beans have to do with telling secrets?" Even knowing the history of a term (if the origin is even known) may not be helpful to some learners. To make things a little more fun, Idiomaginative Explorations has students use AI image generation to bridge the gap between the literal and figurative meanings of idioms. By creating images that combine both the abstract terminology of an idiom and the understood meaning, students will deepen their understanding and retention of these expressions. As the AI in use is unlikely to create the visual image a student is holding in their mind the first time, they will continually reinforce both parts of the idiom as they fine-tune what the picture looks like to create a visual representation of the idiom. This practical approach not only makes learning fun but also enhances creative thinking and digital literacy skills. Here we can encourage students to think critically about language and the meaning of words, providing a different kind of learning experience than they could have had before the advent of AI.

Activity Outline

Setup

- Ensure students have access to the AI image generation tool and understand its basic functions.

- Introduce students to idioms as you normally would in class. This activity doesn't necessarily require idioms to be grouped by theme or any other specialized set of terms. Feel free to incorporate it whenever you are working on idioms with your students.

ISTE STANDARDS
1.1.c / 1.1.d / 1.2.b / 1.2.d / 1.3.b / 1.4.a / 1.5.c / 1.6.b / 1.6.d

RESOURCES
brentgwarner.com/ idiomaginative- explorations

VOCABULARY

Activity

- Students choose an idiom from the list. I recommend a list of about 10 idioms in order to increase the likelihood of multiple students choosing the same idiom, but also ensuring a decent spread of options.

- Students input descriptive prompts into the AI tool to generate an image that represents both the literal and figurative meanings of the idiom.

- Staying in the same chat so that the chatbot remembers what it has been doing, students review and refine their prompts to get the most accurate representation possible.

- In an in-person class, without identifying their chosen idiom, students mingle around the room and present their images to classmates, guessing at the idiom that is meant to align with the image. When they find someone who made an image for a matching idiom, they stay in a group. Students continue this way, building the size of their group until all people with the same idiom are together.

Remind students that pictures won't likely come out perfect the first time. Iterate, iterate, iterate!

- In an online class, prepare breakout rooms and have students search for other people who have a matching idiom. When they find someone with a matching idiom, have them call you in to rename the room in alignment with the idiom. Once a room is renamed, other students with the matching idiom should move to that room, while the rest of the students continue searching for matching partners. Continue until all groups are formed.

Teacher's Role

- Guide students in understanding the idioms and their meanings.

- Assist with technical issues related to the AI tool.

- Provide feedback on the images and help students refine their prompts.

- Listen in during the mingle and encourage students not to just blurt out the name of the idiom, but rather to share the images and have them think critically about what term it might be and how the image represents both the abstract idiom and the true meaning.

Reflection

- Groups should discuss each member's images and how they got the AI to create the specific image. Students should look at each other's work and decide which they think makes the strongest connection between the abstract idiom and the actual meaning.

- There may be some ungrouped students who picked an idiom that nobody else in the class did. In this case, have them join another small group where they can share their unique choice.

Extensions

- Students can create a digital gallery of idiom images. Have them choose the best images and upload them to a shared document that you can embed in your LMS.

- For home explorations, challenge them to make images of different idioms in different artistic styles.

Materials/Tools

Determine whether you need to prepare your own list of idioms or if you'll use ones that are part of a larger class unit. Many teachers like to group idioms by themes, but you are encouraged to determine what is most valuable for your class.

At this point, most AI chatbots like ChatGPT.com and Microsoft Copilot (copilot.microsoft.com) already have some sort of image generator built right in, so as with other AI-related activities in this book, I recommend you work with whatever your school gives you access to. If your school blocks chatbots or there are reasons you can't use open-access AI, remember that Adobe Express (express.adobe.com) and Canva.com also have image generators built-in.

 *Utilize an AI chatbot to review vocabulary through interactive quizzes, cloze activities, and story building.*

ISTE STANDARDS

1.1.b / 1.1.c / 1.1.d / 1.3.b /
1.4.d / 1.5.a / 1.5.c

RESOURCES

brentgwarner.com/
chatvcb

Introduction

ChatVCB uses the flexibility of AI chatbots to create an interactive language learning playground where students can directly review their knowledge of vocabulary through various structured activities. If you're just getting started with AI, vocabulary activities are a great place to test things out as they're fairly easy for teachers to vet, and most vocabulary activities have clear, predictable outcomes (typically, the accurate use or definition of any given word). While students can simply cut and paste the prompts into a chatbot and get started, ChatVCB also introduces them to a bit of prompt engineering by providing a structured prompt that shows a clear outline of what's expected of the interaction. Students will see that it's possible to build interactive, adaptive challenges that cater to individual learning speeds and preferences.

The specific samples provided in the online resources reinforce students' vocabulary through AI-driven exercises such as multiple-choice quizzes, cloze tests, and story creation, and also help them gain confidence in using new words contextually. Still, it's always worth remembering that outputs vary, and the nature of AI is that you can't exactly predict what will be produced. Make sure you talk with your students about this because different platforms may create inconsistent results, and students may need to go through a few iterations with the bot to ensure the expectations and the output match.

Activity Outline

Setup

- Make sure prompts are easily accessible. Prompts for each activity type below are provided in the online resources, but you may want to have them in your LMS where students can easily cut and paste.

- Test the prompts shortly before class. If they are creating unusual output, adjust the prompt to create more consistency. Note that you will never ensure perfect consistency, and that's OK. Uncertainty is part of working with AI.
- Ensure that students have access to the vocabulary words you are working on. An easy place to cut and paste the list (such as in your LMS) will make things easier.

Activity

- Explain the types of review activities students can choose from:
  - Quiz: Students interact with the chatbot to answer a series of multiple-choice questions focused on vocabulary usage.
  - Cloze Activity: Students complete sentences or passages with missing words, guided by contextual clues provided by the chatbot.
  - Story Builder: Students use a set vocabulary list to create stories, aided by the chatbot's suggestions for sentence structure and word choice.
- Students choose which type of review suits their needs. (The activities above go from least to most challenging.)
- Students complete the activity and share the results by submitting a link to their chat.
- If students finish early, they can try a different activity.

Teacher's Role

- Facilitate the activities, provide technical support, and guide students in utilizing the AI chatbot effectively.
- Monitor progress and provide feedback.

Reflection

- Students can grab a partner and share what they learned about the words they've been studying, whether they think there are other ways to use their vocabulary words, and whether they caught the chatbot making mistakes.
- Students who completed more than one activity can write a short evaluation of which activity was more valuable for their review and why.
- Students who focused only on one activity can write a short evaluation of their strengths and weaknesses as discovered through the review process.

VOCABULARY

Extensions

Have students look at the prompts that they cut and pasted into the chatbots. What could they change to make it a better review process that matches their needs? Can they write their own prompt for a completely different type of activity? Challenge them to do so!

Materials/Tools

The title of this activity is a play on ChatGPT, so it should come as no surprise that the activities work well on ChatGPT.com. Still, as mentioned elsewhere in the book, there are many choices, and the tides change from day to day around which is the "best." My advice is to use what you have access to and then explore from there. See AI Chatterbox for more information.

A number of prompts that you can use are provided in the online resources. You are encouraged to use them directly or as inspiration to customize the activities as you see fit.

Expand the Idea—Or Flip It!

THE INFINITE CONTEXT BOT

Students explore and review their vocabulary in use across any topics they are interested in.

Introduction

One of the biggest problems students face when learning new vocabulary words is that they typically study from lists of words completely removed from any context. Even when examples are provided, students typically see only one or two sentences and are expected to figure out the meaning on their own. While we'd all love to give our students endless opportunities to see and interact with vocabulary across different settings and uses, we only have so much time in the day. Or rather, we only had so much time in the day. AI has given us the opportunity to hand our students the keys to the vocab kingdom, and they can explore to their hearts' content in ways that engage, intrigue, and delight them based on their own personal interests.

ISTE STANDARDS
1.1.a / 1.1.b / 1.3.b / 1.3.d

RESOURCES
brentgwarner.com/
theinfinitecontextbot

Activity Outline

Setup

- Prepare a list of vocabulary words that is relevant to the current classroom studies.
- Alternately, have students create their own lists for words they pick up on their own.
- Ensure all students have access to an AI chatbot.

Activity

- Students open the AI chatbot and enter the following prompt:
  - **Prompt:** Assume the role of a materials writer for English Language Learners. I will provide you with a list of vocabulary words I'm working on learning,

VOCABULARY

and you will provide a 2-3 paragraph article using all of the words. My English is at the [CEFR B2] level, so anything you write will be in the same comprehension range. You will suggest 3-4 possible topics that you can write about using the vocabulary words, and you will also add the option for me to choose my own, separate topic. When you're ready, please ask me for the vocabulary list. Wait for my response, then make suggestions for possible topics.

○ Students provide the chatbot with their vocabulary list and decide whether they want to read one of the articles suggested by the chatbot or choose their own separate topic for the chatbot to write about.

○ Students read and analyze the articles, paying attention to how each word is used.

○ Note that at this point you can have students expand the activity in any direction you want. For some teachers, simply having the vocabulary in a variety of contexts is enough. Other teachers may wish to follow some of the suggestions in the Extensions section or create their own expansion activities.

Highlight the importance of critical thinking when analyzing AI-generated content, as the technology may not always produce perfect examples. When I was testing this again during the writing of this chapter, ChatGPT continually gave me unusual uses of the word "convenient" when I asked it to write about how John Carpenter made the movie *Halloween*. While most of the word choices were accurately used, it also said things like "Despite its convenient budget ..." and "... coupled with its convenient yet effective production ..." both of which stood out to me as awkward and something I would highlight for my students.

Teacher's Role

○ Introduce the activity and demonstrate how to use the AI chatbot.

○ Assist students with formulating requests to the chatbot and fine-tuning the topics to get to areas that are truly of interest to the students.

○ Skim and scan the articles created for the students and give them warnings if any of the vocabulary words seem out of place. (Remember, like your students and like all of us, AI doesn't make everything perfectly, and this is a good opportunity to remind students that it's a useful tool, but it can't and won't do all the work for them.)

○ Monitor student progress and provide feedback on their analyses or extensions.

Reflection

○ Inside the same chat, students can ask the chatbot to explain its choices.

- If the teacher skimmed and scanned for unusual word usage and found some, have the students challenge the usage and see what it says.

- In small groups, have students share how they saw words being used in different ways than they were used to.

Extensions

- Have students cut and paste the text into a word processor. Ask them to highlight any examples where the chatbot changed the word form and to explain the change in the comments.

- Consider adjusting the prompt so the chatbot puts out content that matches different styles of writing, for example: opinion pieces, academic writing, children's storybooks, etc.

- Have students ask the chatbot to make a vocabulary quiz based on the content it wrote. You may want to prepare some sample extension prompts depending on the type of quiz you'd like it to create. ChatVCB is a natural way to get started, here.

Materials/Tools

After you have determined the words on your vocabulary list, any chatbot should be able to get this activity going, whether it be ChatGPT.com, Microsoft Copilot (copilot.microsoft.com), or any new bots that come along. As described elsewhere, I recommend that you work with what you have access to and do a couple of dry runs for yourself before handing this activity over to your students. Remember that by their very nature these chatbots create output that varies, so make sure that you're generally aware of what will be made before your lesson begins.

MAGIC PICTURE DICTIONARY

Students create and annotate a digital picture dictionary using AI-generated images to enhance vocabulary retention.

ISTE STANDARDS
1.1.b / 1.1.d / 1.2.c / 1.3.c /
1.6.b / 1.6.c / 1.6.d

RESOURCES
brentgwarner.com/
magicpicturedictionary

Introduction

Picture dictionaries have long been a favorite for beginning students to help memorize basic, everyday vocabulary. But in today's world, students can whip up their own images in styles that appeal to them using simple AI prompts and build their own unique picture dictionaries. Magic Picture Dictionary combines quick AI image generation with simple ways to label the pictures they have created. The ability to make custom images that are culturally relevant to the student can also do a lot to engage them in the learning process. As a broad example, in Japan there are many specific varieties of fish that local people are familiar with, but that are less common or not known overseas. Still, the English names of the fish may be relevant in an EFL context for students who plan to entertain non-Japanese visitors in Japan. Traditional picture dictionaries may never give students the option to learn words to share their own culture, but student-made picture dictionaries can turn that reality on its head.

Once you start generating images to help with vocabulary acquisition, you will find that there are endless possibilities to play with. This version of the activity is focused on helping beginner students develop an understanding of concrete nouns, but as always I encourage you to take the seeds of an idea and let them flourish into your own versions that match your needs.

Activity Outline

Setup
- Prepare a list of vocabulary words related to a theme or lesson.

- Pre-teach the vocabulary and make sure students are generally familiar with the words.

Activity

- Students open the AI image generator and enter the following prompt.

  - **Prompt:** `Create an image of a [LOCATION]. Make the image highly detailed and make sure that all objects in the image are easily distinguishable from one another. In the [LOCATION] please include the following objects: [LIST OF VOCABULARY WORDS]`

    (REMINDER: Before you give this prompt to your students, test it out for yourself and make sure it generally creates what you're looking for on the platform you've chosen. AI is powerful, but not always consistent, so you may need to make adjustments to the prompt to get what you want.)

- Students evaluate the pictures developed and decide whether they are happy with the result, or want to make changes.

  - Most image generators let users fine-tune and change small sections of the image, so if it failed to create wrenches in a garage, a student could highlight the section of the wall and ask it to add wrenches.

  - Sometimes it can be hard to get all the vocabulary words into the image. If students begin to feel frustrated that a few items are missing, encourage them to make separate images for the missing items, or possibly split the vocabulary list in half and make two separate images.

- Students download the image(s) and upload into a slide deck.

- Using the tools in the slide deck, students label the vocabulary.

If students are ambitious but don't have the language they need to create lists for themselves, give them a prompt like this:

Prompt: Give me a list of the 15 most common items I would find in an [Australian] [surf shop]

They could then use this list to supplement the list above and create their own picture dictionary pages to align with their hobbies and interests.

Teacher's Role

- Facilitate the use of the AI tool and slide deck software.

- Project a list of vocabulary words on the screen or write them on the board so students can refer to the list without switching apps on their own computers.

- Provide guidance on vocabulary selection and image interpretation as necessary.

VOCABULARY

Reflection

- Have students compare the image to a setting they are familiar with (their own home, a local shop, a beach they've been to, etc.). Ask them to think through the differences and share any items that they would add to either the generated image or the real place to make the two match more closely. Have them add those vocabulary words to their own vocabulary list.

- Have students discuss with a partner how the images helped them understand and remember the words. If appropriate, have students discuss false cognates and challenge each other to find ways to use the pictures generated to remember the correct meanings of words that sound similar to words in their language.

Extensions

- Students can make copies of their slide decks and remove the vocabulary words they connected to the images. Then they can share a copy of the updated (not filled-out) picture pages with classmates and challenge each other to fill out their respective pages. For an extra challenge, you can have them race to see who can fill out each other's page fastest.

- Students can (and should be encouraged to) revisit and update their dictionaries with new words and images throughout the course. Every time you do this, have students use the same slide deck and simply add new slides. This will make it easier for them to find in the future and it will remind them to review older units every time they open it up!

- Want to add more modalities? Have students record themselves saying the vocabulary words using Vocaroo.com, then insert the audio into the slide deck to play alongside the images.

Materials/Tools

Image generation has become more ubiquitous as the AI revolution has taken root, but the tools all have different quirks. If your school is already in the Microsoft or Google ecosystems, check to see if you and your students have access to Copilot (copilot.microsoft.com) or Gemini (gemini.google.com), respectively. You may also choose to have students use Adobe Express (express.adobe.com) or Canva.com (in which case they don't need to download and upload images into a slide deck as everything is self-contained). If you prefer to avoid the big corporations, a quick search online for "free AI image generator for students" should point you in the right direction.

For your slide decks you have lots of choices. Many students are already familiar with Google Slides (slides.google.com) or Microsoft PowerPoint (powerpoint.office.com), both of which are easy to keep organized and to have students share links to in lieu of uploading files to submit their work.

PHRASAL FRENZY

Students will practice and recall phrasal verbs related to specific topics by competing in teams to complete an online crossword puzzle.

Introduction

Understanding phrasal verbs is crucial for English language learners as they are commonly used in everyday English. They also tend to be one of the areas where students struggle the most as different teachers approach teaching them in different ways (by primary verb, by prepositional phrase, etc.). Unfortunately, there are simply too many variables to accommodate every grammatical approach to phrasal verbs, so instead this activity focuses on a simple review strategy of words students have already been practicing.

In fact, decades of research show that crossword puzzles can increase student engagement, boost confidence, and reinforce definitions of words and spelling. With this in mind, Phrasal Frenzy uses online crossword puzzles to create a fun way to help students review and remember phrasal verbs by their overall meaning. Instead of breaking down the phrasal verbs into individual words, this approach encourages students to focus on the holistic meaning of each verb phrase. By categorizing the phrasal verbs into themes like "Business," "Money," or "Love," students can contextualize their learning, making it more practical and relevant. Adding in a competitive twist motivates students to work together and quickly recall phrasal verbs, enhancing their vocabulary retention and usage in real-life conversations.

ISTE STANDARDS
1.1.c / 1.3.b / 1.6.d / 1.7.b

RESOURCES
brentgwarner.com/
phrasalfrenzy

Activity Outline

Setup

- Teachers create a list of phrasal verbs based on a specific topic (e.g., "Business").

- Use an online crossword creator to create a crossword puzzle using these phrasal verbs.

- Divide the class into small teams and if you're teaching in-person, ensure each team has access to a computer or tablet with internet.

VOCABULARY

Activity

- Introduce the topic and provide a brief explanation of the chosen phrasal verbs.
- Share the link to the crossword puzzle with each team.
- Explain the rules: the first team to complete the crossword puzzle correctly wins.
- Start the competition and use a timer to track progress.
- Teams work together to complete the crossword puzzle, focusing on the meanings of the phrasal verbs.
  - Remember that winning teams don't need elaborate prizes. High fives work just as well as candy, and avoiding the extra credit game may help shift learning motivation away from extrinsic rewards and toward intrinsic satisfaction.

Teacher's Role

- Facilitate the initial discussion on the chosen topic and phrasal verbs.
- Assist teams in navigating the crossword website.
- Provide hints or additional explanations if teams struggle with certain phrasal verbs.
- Monitor the competition and ensure fair play.

Reflection

- After the competition, have a class discussion where students share which phrasal verbs were challenging and why. If necessary, break down any confusing or problematic definitions that slowed groups down.
- Encourage students to use the phrasal verbs in sentences to demonstrate their understanding.

Extensions

- Teams can create dialogues incorporating the phrasal verbs. For more advanced classes, have the dialogues reinforce the phrasal verbs by clarifying with the definitions.
- Revisit the activity with different topics to expand students' vocabulary further.

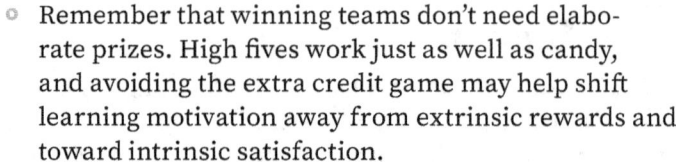

This activity is a great way to move a traditional paper-based activity to classes that meet online. Of course, there's no reason you couldn't simply print out the crossword puzzle and have students do it on paper. There's no reason to use tech just for tech's sake—determine what works best for you and your class and make the adjustments necessary!

Creating crossword lists used to be a time-consuming affair, but with the use of AI chatbots you can have endless lists made for you in a flash. Need help making a list of words? Here's a quick prompt you can plug into any chatbot to help you out:

Prompt: Create a list of 10 phrasal verbs about romantic relationships that are at the [CEFR A2 level]. Each phrasal verb should be followed by a brief (2–3 word) definition.

Materials/Tools

Like other activities throughout the book that require a vocabulary list of sorts, I encourage you to create a list of phrasal verbs that is relevant to what your students are studying in class. Some teachers may find that requires building a new list (see side note), while others may have something readily available.

There are a lot of online crossword creators out there, but for many years the majority of them only made printable puzzles—not particularly useful if you're trying to have students collaborate online. In more recent years, though, excellent resources have been developed that allow you to create both online and printable versions of puzzles, finally bringing these classic games into the modern world.

CrosswordLabs.com is a user-friendly tool for creating custom crossword puzzles. It allows teachers to input vocabulary lists and generate puzzles that students can complete online. It's a great option if you want to give students a quick link. AmuseLabs.com lets you build games and embed them right into your LMS, so if you want to keep everything in a single ecosystem, it's a great choice.

Depending on your sense of showmanship, you may want to project a timer with pretty graphics (many are readily available on YouTube), or you may simply use the timer built into Google by typing "stopwatch" into the search bar. Of course, the timer in your phone, or an old-fashioned handheld timer works, too.

CORPUS CLASH

 *Utilize an online corpus to explore word usage in context, enhancing vocabulary and tech skills through competitive activities.*

ISTE STANDARDS
1.1.c / 1.3.a / 1.3.b /
1.5.b / 1.6.d

RESOURCES
brentgwarner.com/
corpusclash

Introduction

A corpus is a large database of texts (newspapers, books, transcripts, etc.) that linguists and other researchers use to understand language patterns, grammar, and more. While many teachers shy away from the use of a corpus, finding them overwhelming, there are very few resources that do such a good job of letting students get a clear view of the real usage of the English language across different media. Corpus Clash takes advantage of the rich data of English-Corpora.org to turn vocabulary learning into a lightly competitive, engaging classroom activity. By integrating simple corpus searches, students get a chance to expand their vocabulary and gain insights into real-world language use. Further, the game introduces students to corpus linguistics—a key tool in language learning and research—through a format that encourages exploration and critical thinking. The competitive element can be a fun way to stimulate deeper engagement with the material while providing a practical, hands-on way to understand word frequencies, collocations, and context.

A corpus is a tool that many students are unaware of and the look on their faces when they start to discover the power is one of the reasons we all teach. In my own experiences, many students have come back to talk to me long after they left the class, and they continue to thank me for introducing them to the corpus resources we used. Keep in mind my first warning, though: When you first introduce a corpus, keep things simple as pushing into further interactions can quickly start to feel like a computer programming class!

Activity Outline

Setup

- Brief students on how to access and perform basic searches on a corpus.

- Prepare a list of commonly used words with multiple meanings. Note that the right vocabulary list makes this game work and it may not align with vocabulary lists you have for other purposes. I've provided some samples for various levels in the online resources.

Activity

- Divide students into teams.

- Project a word for the class. Teams will search the corpus for the word.

- Each team needs to find three different samples of the word being used with one decided meaning. For example, if students search for the word "break" and provide two samples where it means "to smash, split, or divide" and one sample where it means "a brief rest," they would not be successful.

  - Students can copy and paste the examples onto a document or write them on a piece of paper.

- When the team agrees they've found three matching examples, they need to define the vocabulary in their own words and create an original sentence using it with the same meaning.

- When they are ready, all team members raise their hands.

- The teacher tracks the order of raised hands, then waits for all teams to raise their hands (You may consider a time limit of three to five minutes—adjust to your class level and needs).

- The first team presents their findings first, and points are distributed as follows:

  - Original Definition (a meaning not used by another team): 2 points

  - Repeated Definition (another group used the same meaning and raised their hands first): 1 point

Struggling to find the right words? Try a simple prompt like this to help you out:

Prompt: I'm looking for a list of 10 vocabulary words that have multiple meanings and can cause confusion for English Language Learners. The words should be at the [CEFR A2] level. Please add 2–3 quick definitions for each word to ensure that the meanings are clearly distinct.

Note that this activity can take time, so you may limit speaking groups to the first two or three to complete the activity, or if you pre-judged results, the first few who selected different definitions for the words.

This activity can be a springboard for more advanced corpus research projects. If this is your goal, make sure you train yourself on the corpus you expect your students to use.

- 3-way Match (all three samples use the same meaning): 2 points
- Mismatch (one of the samples provided had a different meaning of the word than the other two): 1 point
- Correct Sample (Student-made sentence uses the word correctly): 1 point
  - Continue with the next word.

Teacher's Role

- Help students log into the corpus and understand how to search.
- During presentations, evaluate the relevancy and uniqueness of examples.
- Award points as necessary.
  - *Tip:* To save time, you may do a check-in on groups as they raise their hand, and determine how many points they get before they present.

Reflection

- As a class, students discuss which meanings they were previously unfamiliar with. Ask students to share which other groups' definitions or sample sentences helped them better understand the vocabulary.

Extensions

- Students write short stories incorporating as many of the different definitions of the vocabulary as possible.
- As homework, students can be challenged to find sample sentences for meanings that were not discussed/discovered in class.

Materials/Tools

The primary tool is English-Corpora.org, though there are other corpora available. English Corpora (corpora is the plural of corpus) is the most widely used and accesses the most popular corpora including the Corpus of Contemporary American English (COCA), The British National Corpus (BNC), and many more. If you wanted to focus on more informal English, you could use the TV Corpus or the Movie Corpus, all of which are accessible through the same website.

While Corpus Clash was designed with English Corpora in mind, there's no reason you can't use any corpus that you have access to. Many universities have access to their own databases, so check what's available to you. Further, if you're using this book to help students learn languages other than English, you may find that existing corpora in your language have a similar layout making this activity easily transferrable.

ANTONYMS ON A LOG

Students work together to arrange gradable antonyms on a spectrum to enhance vocabulary understanding and usage.

Introduction

Gradable antonyms—words that express varying degrees of a quality, such as freezing > chilly > cool > tepid > warm > toasty > hot—are a great way to get students to expand their vocabulary and increase their accuracy in communication. By using a digital whiteboard, students can work together to figure out where these words stand in relation to one another according to their intensity. This process bolsters vocabulary comprehension and sharpens analytical thinking as students evaluate nuances between words. Doing this on a shared digital whiteboard allows students to both learn from and challenge one another (though you may want to break it down into smaller groups just to keep things manageable). Once students have a sense of how the words stand in relation to one another, you can move into all sorts of production-based activities where they can demonstrate their comprehension.

ISTE STANDARDS
1.1.c / 1.1.d / 1.2.d / 1.3.b / 1.3.d

RESOURCES
brentgwarner.com/
antonymsonalog

Activity Outline

Setup

- Provide a list of gradable antonyms such as the freezing > hot example provided above, or any that suit your needs.

- Prepare a digital whiteboard with a horizontal line representing a spectrum as well as digital cards with the vocabulary words to be manipulated.

- *Note:* Feel free to make a copy of the template in the online resources and repurpose for your needs.

VOCABULARY

- Using your LMS, distribute the whiteboard to your students either as a single class whiteboard (this could get wild, but I'm not discouraging a little fun!), or to groups.

Activity

- In pairs or small groups, students discuss and place the antonyms along the spectrum based on their intensity or degree.
- Challenge students to bunch word cards in clusters depending on how similar they are to one another. For example, if you're talking about height, they might put the cards for "average" and "normal" right on top of one another, where "tall" might end up further down the line and "gigantic" might be at the very far end.

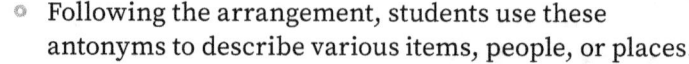

  - Following the arrangement, students use these antonyms to describe various items, people, or places.

Teacher's Role

- If students are meant to discover meaning on their own, determine the types of hints you're willing to provide.
- Circle the groups and give feedback on pronunciation for any unfamiliar word.
- Provide feedback on their choices and descriptions.

Reflection

- Students reflect on their learning by writing a short paragraph using the gradable antonyms to describe a familiar scenario or object.

Extensions

- Beginner students can be encouraged to add their L1 equivalents to words. Note that sometimes they may find they don't have an equivalent in their first language, which is always a good opportunity for linguistic discovery!
- Introduce more complex or less common gradable antonyms, or have students create their own examples of gradable antonyms after you've provided two extremes (e.g. sad-happy).

This activity can be adapted for different proficiency levels by varying the complexity of the antonyms. This works both in remote and in-class settings.

For a no-tech version, simply draw a line across the whiteboard, then place a bunch of sticky notes with the words around the board and ask students to arrange the sticky notes.

Examples of gradable antonyms to use might include "quiet-noisy," "bright-dark," "light-heavy," "slow-fast," "infant-senior," each with multiple intermediate points that students can explore and define.

Materials/Tools

There are a lot of digital whiteboards out there that you can work with. Some teachers like to stick with Google Slides (slides.google.com), as they're fairly simple, while others like more sophisticated tools like Miro.com or Microsoft Whiteboard (edushare.ing/MSWhiteboard). One of the popular choices recently has been FigJam (figma.com/figjam), which allows for a lot of customization and is free for students and teachers. I'll admit that setting up a FigJam board does have a bit of a learning curve, but many teachers love the flexibility.

Challenge: Supplement These Ideas With Your Own Doodles

WORDS IN THE WILD

Students will hunt and capture real-world instances of vocabulary words.

ISTE STANDARDS
1.1.b / 1.1.d / 1.2.a /
1.2.c / 1.3.d / 1.6.b /
1.6.c / 1.6.d / 1.7.b

RESOURCES
brentgwarner.com/
wordsinthewild

Introduction

Words in the Wild transforms vocabulary learning into an adventurous scavenger hunt, where students are tasked with tracking down words in their natural habitats—whether urban jungles or painted plains. Armed only with their digital cameras (smartphones, tablets), students shoot images of vocabulary words found in contexts such as billboards, menus, and magazines, and then share their treasures with the rest of the class. This activity encourages students to keep their vocabulary at front of mind even outside of class. Depending on your setting, this may be possible as an activity completed during class time, but you'll probably prefer to make it an opportunity for home exploration after the school bell rings.

To keep things entertaining, you can add all sorts of gamification dynamics to the hunt. You could offer extra points (perhaps referred to as "prize money") to the best hunter, who might get bonuses for being the first one to find a word, or perhaps certain vocabulary that's less common is worth more. Further, you could incentivize students to do more reading by offering more for finding examples in print books and magazines, where possibly digital examples (easily found with a quick CTRL+F) would be worth much less. You have endless flexibility with what you ask students to do on top of this simple framework. For more info on how to gamify your activities, look at *Power Up Your Classroom* (iste.org/PowerUpClassroom) by Lindsey Blass and Cate Tolnai.

Activity Outline

Setup

- Determine the level of gamification you want to apply to the activity. Is the goal simply to find the words and share them (simple can be best depending on the situation!), or do you want to build some extrinsic motivation and opportunities for collaboration and/or competition?

○ Assign vocabulary words to students.

○ Explain the requirement of finding these words in real-world contexts like magazines, billboards, menus, or books.

Activity

○ Students keep an eye out for their vocabulary words in use in the wild.

　• Note that if you span this over a week or two, they may need reminders, especially at the beginning. If this is a continuous activity you maintain over the semester, the need to remind them will dissipate over time as it becomes a part of their routine.

○ Upload photos to a designated online platform where the class can see each other's finds.

Teacher's Role

○ Monitor the uploads for appropriateness and completeness.

○ Send reminders to students so they train themselves to keep an eye out. You can use the announcement feature on your LMS, a class chatroom, or a service like Remind.com.

○ Assign points if you're gamifying the activity, or consider asking students to keep track of their own points if you've laid out clear ground rules.

○ Provide feedback and encouragement, facilitate discussions around the context of the usage and the nuances of the language.

If needed, consider setting specific guidelines on privacy and digital etiquette, especially regarding taking pictures in public places or of people.

Making this a group assignment may reduce the burden to keep this activity in mind all the time. It would also encourage students to think about the words and to be in touch with each other about the vocabulary several times throughout the week, reenforcing the learning every time.

Reflection

○ At the end of the week (perhaps just before a quiz), open a classroom discussion about the most interesting or surprising contexts where they or their classmates found the words.

Extensions

○ Students can connect the photos together to write a short story about a "day around town" that also incorporates the vocabulary. If they find some of their own photos don't work well for the story they want to tell, perhaps they can use some of the photos their classmates used instead.

Materials/Tools

Options for how you want to collect images are infinite and can be as organized or as loose as you like. For many teachers, the easiest option may be to use the message board system built right into your LMS. This doesn't cost any extra and keeps both the teacher and students in a platform everyone is already familiar with. Some message boards allow for subtopics, so you might consider making the main topic the week or unit you are working on, and the subtopics could be each respective vocabulary word, under which students would post their pictures.

If you want to go a little looser, many of your students are already using Discord.com to communicate with one another for gaming and live streaming. There's a bit of a learning curve here if you're new to it, but there's real power in being where your students already are. Once you get the hang of things, it's fairly easy to set up channels where you could ask students to post their shots.

If you're more of a highly organized type, Padlet.com is a great platform for this that could easily be organized to allow users to collaborate and post content in a visually organized bulletin board. This may be a great choice for many as the layout is clear and it supports image uploads and text comments directly from a phone. See Fiberoptic Fishbowl Forum for more info on Padlet.

Don't Let This Space go to Waste!

Pronunciation

Language and accents govern so much of how people think about other people.

— TREVOR NOAH

Pronunciation, accents, intonations and everything else that falls under the category of how we say things versus what we say are not only great ways to bridge comprehension and effective communication, they're also an excellent opportunity for us to help students understand the nuance of language and the personality of those who use it.

Over the last several years, especially with the release of AI chatbots, there have been a lot of new opportunities for students to build their pronunciation skills without a teacher holding their hand through the entire process. Language learners now have better access to resources that offer individualized practice, immediate feedback, and the opportunity to learn pronunciation in a less intimidating environment than many may be comfortable with.

Several times throughout the activities and online resources, I reference the idea that your pronunciation may not be the same as mine, so please make sure to adjust the assignments and resources as needed. Of course, this is true for English speakers across the globe, but I also want to recognize that world language teachers who are using this book to build activities for their own language class will have to make extra accommodations to incorporate these activities. I recommend focusing on the framework and planning to build out your own content.

Remember that it's hard to separate pronunciation from speaking, so as you move through these activities consider how you can integrate them with activities in the speaking chapter or with your own assignments.

INVESTIGATED, USED, AND DISCUSSED

Students practice and improve their pronunciation of the -ed endings in past tense verbs through peer feedback in an online setting.

ISTE STANDARDS

1.1.c / 1.1.d / 1.2.b / 1.6.d

RESOURCES

brentgwarner.com/
investigatedused-
anddiscussed

Introduction

This is a simple way for students in an online setting to practice their pronunciation either with partners in breakout rooms or in front of the whole class. Many students struggle with distinguishing the different *-ed* ending sounds of past tense verbs. It's easy enough to remember the rules (words that end in *d* or *t* have a fully pronounced syllable of /Id/, words that end in a vowel sound or voiced consonant end in a /d/ sound, and verbs that end in an unvoiced consonant end in a /t/ sound with no extra syllable). Harder though, is producing these sounds. Regular and reinforced practice is important here, and in an online class it's an easy activity to have students practice. With cameras off and audio on, students can speak words while the classmates or teachers give them feedback on what they heard. Listeners can type what they heard into the chat box so speakers get a fair and honest representation of what their classmates heard from them, allowing them to quickly make adjustments as necessary to speak the words clearly.

Activity Outline

Setup

- Teach the distinction between the three different *-ed* pronunciations at the end of verbs.

- Prepare a list of verbs that will elicit different *-ed* pronunciations.

- Determine whether you want to make this a pair/small group or a whole class activity. If you're working in pairs or groups, prepare breakout rooms.

- Instruct students to have their cameras off and audio on.

Activity

- If working as a full-class activity, call on a volunteer to be the speaker. Everyone else will be listeners.

- If working in pairs or small groups, ensure that students choose a speaker when they enter breakout rooms. Send them to breakout rooms.

- The speaker will turn off their camera so the listeners focus on what they hear.

- Provide the speaker with a list of verbs written in the past tense and have them slowly say each of the words.

- Listeners type the pronunciation they think they heard into the chat box: "id," "t," or "d." So if the speaker is given the word "walked" and they pronounce it as "walk-ed" the listeners would type "id". Important: Remind listeners to type in what they hear, and not what the correct pronunciation is (if they happen to know it).

- After each turn, students receive feedback from their peers and adjust their pronunciation as needed.

- Rotate roles so each student gets a chance to speak and listen.

Teacher's Role

- Monitor pronunciation or breakout rooms to provide support and ensure engagement.

- Offer additional feedback and clarification on pronunciation rules as needed.

- Act as the final judge in cases where students disagree.

Reflection

- Have students take note of the sounds they found challenging and determine if there is a pattern in the words they are mispronouncing. For example, they might recognize that they have a habit of using the /Id/ sound with every word that ends with /k/ even though they do pretty well with other unvoiced consonants.

Students can do this very easily in class by simply having students hold their hand in front of their mouth, removing all need for tech.

Of course this works for all pronunciation activities, so feel free to focus on whatever issue your students are dealing with.

This activity really does need humans working together. Unlike some other speaking or pronunciation activities, speaking these words incorrectly into an AI transcription service or dictation tool will likely autocorrect the word to the correct spelling. You may find some examples where an /ɪd/ pronunciation after "watch" will auto-transcribe to "watch it," but I wouldn't count on it to be as reliable for feedback as another human as speech-to-text tools are not built with supporting pronunciation issues in mind.

PRONUNCIATION

Extensions

- Instead of using individual vocabulary words, have students read out full sentences with verbs in the past tense. Challenge them to see if they have the same pronunciation struggles with words when they're embedded in sentences as when they are by themselves.

Materials/Tools

The only thing you need here is a meeting platform like Zoom.com, Google Meet (meet.google.com), Discord.com, etc. With the "camera on or off" debate still happening for teachers around the world, at least this is one time everyone can agree the point is to have the camera off and listen in. Since most meeting platforms also have a chat box installed, any service you use should be a great all-in-one solution.

If available, headphones with microphones built in will usually provide significantly higher quality recordings than the microphone built into a phone or computer.

Got Other Ideas? Write 'Em Here!

SOUND SYMBOL MEMORY MATCH

Students will accurately match spoken sounds to their corresponding IPA symbols to improve pronunciation and phonetic awareness.

Introduction

If you've ever taught the International Phonetic Alphabet (IPA), you've no doubt used all sorts of charts to help students match sounds to symbols. The problems with these kinds of charts, traditionally, is that students may see that the word "green" uses the /i/ sound, but their own pronunciation of "green" may be affected by transfer from their first language. There are a lot of good websites where students can listen to the correct sounds, but not a lot of them are designed to help memorize and reinforce the correct sounds with the symbols.

Sound Symbol Memory Match is a very basic card-flip memory game that takes advantage of being in a digital space to add multimedia, particularly audio that can be vetted by the teacher. By pairing audible words with their IPA symbols, students can develop a keen ear for the actual sounds they are supposed to master. Utilizing digital flash-cards also means that students can practice on their own at home or in the library without you as the teacher to check in and reinforce the pronunciation every time. This activity supports auditory discrimination, reinforces phonetic symbols, and provides a solid foundation for accurate pronunciation.

Activity Outline

Setup

- If conducting the activity in class, provide headphones for clear listening. Failure to do so will result in a cacophony of sounds that will only lead to unbridled chaos.

ISTE STANDARDS

1.1.c / 1.1.d / 1.3.b / 1.5.c

RESOURCES

brentgwarner.com/ soundsymbol- memorymatch

PRONUNCIATION

- Create a set of digital flashcards that pair sounds with their corresponding IPA symbols.
- Consider the level of your class and the types of sounds you want them to focus on.
- Keep in mind that having too many cards makes it very difficult for people to find matches.

Activity

- Students open the digital flashcard set on their device.
- They flip a card and either listen to the sound or check the IPA symbol.
- They flip through other flashcards to find the corresponding IPA symbol or sound to their first card.
- If they find a match, cards will disappear from the screen.
  - If they do not find a match, cards will flip back over and students will try again.
  - Students continue this process, working to correctly match all sounds and symbols until the screen is clear.

Teacher's Role

- Introduce the activity, reinforcing the value of hearing the actual sounds rather than students imagining the sounds in their heads.
- Monitor students' progress, providing assistance as needed.

Reflection

- Students can discuss which sounds were challenging and how they improved their listening skills.

Extensions

- For some light competition, consider having a race to see who can finish fastest.
- Put students in pairs and create a rule that each can only click once per round and enforce a "no pointing at the screen" rule.

To support your students, there are many interactive IPA charts available online. Over the years I've found that different teachers take a liking to any number of different sites for their own reasons, so please take the time to explore. One simple option is ipachart.com, a wonderful resource that plays audible phonemes of isolated consonant and vowel sounds; just prepare yourself for lots of weird groans and grunts to come out of your students' computers when they start clicking around.

Materials/Tools

By far my favorite (and free!) way to do this is by using Flippity.net. It works by accessing a Google Sheet (sheets.google.com) spreadsheet and converting the content into interactive activities on a public-facing website. All you have to do is customize the content on a Google Sheet (provided to you by Flippity) and then share the link to the website with your students. For the Matching Game activity in Flippity, there is also an option to auto-speak from 16 different languages or accents, as well as an option to plug in your own audio files if you want to focus on regional dialects.

There are plenty of other options out there like puzzel.org, and while not all are free, they may offer upgrades or features that appeal to you.

Keep in mind that in a classroom setting, trying to distinguish sounds can get hard when 25 other classmates are playing their own audio. Headphones can immediately alleviate any problems that might come up from "stray" sounds bouncing across the room.

Here's Your Remix Zone

MINIMAL PAIRS CASCADE

Students will practice distinguishing and pronouncing minimal pairs through an interactive listening and speaking activity.

ISTE STANDARDS

1.1.a / 1.1.c / 1.2.b / 1.6.b

RESOURCES

brentgwarner.com/
minimalpairscascade

Introduction

Minimal Pairs Cascade involves one student speaking out words from a selection of minimal pairs while the rest of the class mentally moves through a cascading chart based on the words they hear. It encourages active listening and provides immediate feedback on their pronunciation accuracy. By rotating roles, students get the chance to practice both speaking and listening, reinforcing their learning through peer interaction. This activity not only makes pronunciation practice enjoyable but also enhances students' confidence in speaking English.

At its core, this is a very low-tech activity that you can layer tech onto as you become more comfortable with different tools. In fact, I've used this activity for years just by drawing circles on a board, but it can also be used as a fun way to onboard students into basic technology use in the classroom, so jump down to the Extensions section for ideas on how to digitize the game.

Activity Outline

Setup

- Prepare the Minimal Pairs Cascade chart and ensure each student has access to it.
- Prepare a list of minimal pairs for the activity.
- Arrange students in groups and assign the first speaker.

Activity

- The speaker chooses a word from each minimal pair list and says it out loud.
- Listeners move down the chart based on what they hear (left for one word, right for the other).
- After moving through the entire chart, students note their final position (#1–#16).
- The speaker reveals the correct words, and listeners compare their positions.
- Rotate roles, allowing a new student to be the speaker and repeat the process.
- After a few students have spoken in front of the class, you can break them into small groups where they can continue the activity huddled together, ensuring everyone has a chance to speak.

Teacher's Role

- Ensure students understand the discrete differences between minimal pairs.
- Teach the class how to move down the chart.
- Monitor pronunciation and provide feedback.
- Rotate students to the front of the class to try their hand at pronouncing the words.
- Encourage students to speak clearly and listen attentively.

Reflection

- After each round, students discuss any discrepancies in their positions. If most students landed on the same final number, it's a good indication that the speaker spoke clearly and perhaps a few students weren't paying close attention. With some experience, the teacher and the class will start to see patterns of individual words that might have been problematic.
- Review common pronunciation challenges and strategies to improve.

Minimal Pairs: Word pairs differing by only one sound, changing meaning, like "rock" and "lock."

Emphasize the importance of clear pronunciation and active listening.

Use a variety of minimal pairs to cover different sounds and increase difficulty progressively.

Encourage a supportive environment where students feel comfortable making mistakes and learning from them.

Extensions

- As mentioned before, Minimal Pairs Cascade can be as low-tech as a chalkboard, but you can build on top of it with tools as you and the class become more comfortable with technology.

- If you want students to focus on their listening distinction skills, one option is to record your own voice speaking different paths through the end. Students can then submit the final answer they heard from you through the LMS, Google Forms, or any other method. For some classes, this may help students prepare to do the speaking the next time class is in session.

- In Padlet, you can upload the chart and have students record their own voice speaking through it. Students can then respond to classmates, letting them know where they ended up on the chart.

Materials/Tools

Fundamentally, all you need is a slide deck and a way to project it. You can copy my sample template from the online resources and duplicate as needed to align with the minimal pairs you're working on.

If you're moving into the extensions, you can record audio of your voice on a free computer program or using an online service like Vocaroo.com. As mentioned above, there are endless ways to extend, including using tools such as Google Forms (forms.google.com), Microsoft Forms (forms.office.com), Padlet.com, and more.

Doodle Break Encouraged!

SAY IT RIGHT

Enhance students' pronunciation skills through a fun and competitive race using tech-based feedback.

Introduction

We've all played games where students have to run to the front of the class to complete a task and then pass off the torch to another group member until all group members have played. Say it Right takes this structure and equalizes the judging while helping students learn where to pinpoint changes in their pronunciation. Using a computer-generated analysis, students receive immediate feedback on their pronunciation while they move through a list of words. This game motivates students to practice diligently and collaborate with their peers, aiming to be the first team to correctly pronounce all the words on the list. As with any game of this sort, there are all sorts of ways to make adjustments. By putting the list of words on display, students in waiting can discuss their playing order and play when a word they are more confident with comes up. If a student really doesn't want to play, consider bringing them up as a judge to confirm the computer's feedback.

Activity Outline

Setup

- Set up three laptops at the front of the classroom. Try to space them as far apart as possible so they don't pick up other people's voices when recording.

- Prepare a list of words to pronounce and project it on the board. Your words may be focused on a particular sound you're working on in class, or they could be a broader review of how to pronounce vocabulary words you've been learning.

- Divide students into three teams and have them wait together at the back of the class. This explanation assumes a class of roughly 30 students practicing 10 words (10 students per group, each completing the challenge once), but you can change the numbers to fit your needs.

ISTE STANDARDS
1.1.c / 1.3.b / 1.6.b / 1.7.c

RESOURCES
brentgwarner.com/
sayitright

PRONUNCIATION

Activity

- The first student from each team goes to the front and types "How to pronounce [word]" into Google Search. This should open a pronunciation field that includes a button to listen to the pronunciation and a practice button to try your own hand at the pronunciation.

- Students listen to the pronunciation and attempt to pronounce the word using the practice button and their microphone.

- If Google says "Good job!" the student raises their hand to signal the teacher.

- Once confirmed by the teacher, the student returns to their team, and the next player goes up to try the next word.

- If a student cannot get the pronunciation right, they can pass, and another team member can try.

- The next student types in "How to pronounce [next word]" into the search box, then repeat the process above.

- The team that correctly pronounces all the words on the list first wins.

Want your students to be better prepared? Have them practice the list of words the night before the activity for homework.

Foster a supportive and positive competitive environment to ensure all students feel motivated and included. Remind students that sometimes the microphone doesn't pick up sounds well, and it even tells native speakers that their pronunciation was wrong.

Consider incorporating this activity into a broader speaking skills curriculum to maximize its impact.

Teacher's Role

- Project the list of words and demonstrate how to use the Google Search "how to pronounce" function.

- Confirm correct pronunciations when students raise their hands.

- Keep track of time and ensure fair play.

- Encourage and support all teams, providing feedback as necessary.

Reflection

- After the game, have a class discussion about which words were the most challenging and what strategies helped.

- On their own, students should go through the list and try to practice all the words. Have them take note of any repeated feedback they get. For example, if it regularly tells them they are using the /p/ sound instead of the /f/ sound, this is a good area to work on in the future.

PRONUNCIATION

Extensions

- Instead of having all groups move to the front of the class, you could have each team stand behind their representative. This way they could coach and encourage each other if the pronunciation is a struggle. Note that this approach could get loud quickly, so you might make a rule where everyone except the speaker has to whisper.

- If you want to move away from an all-or-nothing approach, you could give a point spread, for example: Three points for a word spoken correctly the first time, two points for a word spoken correctly the second time, one point for a word with an error in the second attempt, etc. Again, it's endlessly flexible to your needs, your students' abilities, and the amount of time you have in class!

Materials/Tools

You may need a little preparation time, so make sure you have a way to set up three computers in front of the classroom. Most teachers will probably slide chairs and desks to the front of the class, but your setting may require doing things differently. While you're at it, double check that each computer has a working microphone and functional speakers.

While there are a number of pronunciation tools available and more and more are getting better with feedback thanks to AI, the Google pronunciation tool has been a free but hidden gem for years, and the fact that it has no login and is easily accessible on the Google.com homepage makes it the primary tool I recommend for this game. To access it, you simply type "How to pronounce [word]" directly into the Google search. Note that these features may not show up in every region, so test it out for yourself first.

SPEAK AND SEE

Students work to improve their pronunciation by using voice typing to practice specific sounds, sentences, and minimal pairs.

Introduction

A lot of traditional pronunciation practice has focused on listening and repeating, then trying to keep the sounds straight in students' heads. Luckily, advancements in technology means that we can use pretty impressive voice recognition tools that are built right into our word processors to help visualize our pronunciation. When students can see that the utterances they are verbalizing are being typed onto the screen and those written words are the very words they were trying to say, a sense of satisfaction overcomes them in a way that the teacher saying, "Good job!" just doesn't cover.

Speak and See leverages these dictation tools to provide immediate feedback on pronunciation accuracy. By focusing on specific sounds, similar sentences, and minimal pairs (or whatever you like, really), students can target challenging areas and see real-time results. In my own classes, I've seen students take this activity and practice it with articles and stories they like—not for homework, just for their own practice. For many students, this not only makes pronunciation practice interactive and engaging but also allows them to self-assess and make necessary corrections.

Activity Outline

Setup

○ Ensure students' computers are able to activate the microphone. Note that it will be helpful for you to have basic proficiency to do this on Windows, Macs, and Chromebooks, but if you're not sure and one student is struggling, there's usually another student in the class who can help them out.

○ Prepare a document focusing on specific sounds, sentences, or minimal pairs. See online resources for a sample.

ISTE STANDARDS
1.1.c / 1.2.b / 1.3.b

RESOURCES
brentgwarner.com/speakandsee

- Distribute the document through your LMS or however you prefer students to get digital documents.

Activity

- Students open the document.
- Individually, students review the words and phrases provided.
- When they are ready, they activate the voice typing tool in their word processor.
- Students click into the aligning table cells and one by one, read the words or phrases aloud, aiming to match the pronunciation shown on the document.
- The voice typing tool will transcribe their speech, allowing students to see if they pronounced the words correctly.
- If some words or phrases don't show up as the word they are trying to say, encourage students to try again or call you over if they're struggling.

Teacher's Role

- Prepare and share documents tailored to the pronunciation needs of the class.
- Demonstrate how to use the voice typing tool.
- Provide feedback and additional practice for students struggling with specific sounds.

Reflection

- Students compare their transcriptions with the provided words and phrases.
- Have them note areas of difficulty and practice those sounds further.
- Encourage them not to delete the old, incorrect versions, but instead to try again and dictate underneath their old output. They don't have to do this indefinitely, but it can help them see progress or changes the voice analyzer is picking up on.
- Students can share their experiences and improvements with the class.

In the modern era, I've seen a lot of students trying to complete work like this in school hallways, outdoor food courts, or with TVs blasting in the background. Make sure to reinforce that a quiet recording space will do a lot to help the student know if any problems are due to their pronunciation, or interference from background noises.

This activity can be adapted for different proficiency levels by varying the complexity of the words and phrases.

Extensions

- Students can create their own pronunciation practice documents for themselves or their peers.
- Incorporate more complex sentences or paragraphs as students progress.
- Students use the tool to practice pronunciation in different contexts, such as reading aloud from books or scripts.

Materials/Tools

Dictation tools are common across all the major word processors (and probably across all the minor ones at this point, too); the trick is in knowing where to find them. Whether you've got students working on school-issued Windows machines, their own fancy Macs, or logging into Google Docs (docs.google.com), there should be a way to have them participate.

In Google Docs, the feature is called "Voice Typing," and you can find it under the "Tools" menu along the top bar. When you click on "Voice Typing," a little pop-up box will appear with a microphone that your students can then click to begin their dictation.

In Microsoft Word (Microsoft.com/Word), the feature is called "Dictate," and you can find it under the "Home" menu bar. Look along the bar until you find the microphone icon. A settings feature is also included in the Word dictation pop-up, which might be worth perusing.

In Apple Pages (edushare.ing/ApplePages), you can find the feature called "Start Dictation" under the "Edit" menu bar drop-down. Apple's pop-up is the least intrusive, just a small icon where your typing cursor sits, but unfortunately the pop-up doesn't stay immediately available when you want to turn it off. If your students are Mac users, I recommend you teach them the hot key "fn+D" to quickly toggle the dictation on and off.

A STRESS-FULL QUIZ

Students identify the correct stress patterns in multisyllabic words using a quizzing platform.

Introduction

One part of pronunciation I've always loved teaching is stress. Students can have a ton of fun playing with the sounds of words and in some full-body exercises jumping around or swaying their bodies to represent where the stress lies in a given word. It's also important to remind them that misplacing stress in words can lead to misunderstandings and affect fluency. While many teachers like to incorporate specific rules around which words are stressed in English, it's easy to find endless exceptions. Because of this, it might be worth talking about the tendencies of stress rather than hard and fast rules, as suggested by Adrien Underhill, accomplished editor of many English language teaching books. Once students start to get the hang of things, you can use A Stress-Full Quiz to give students a fun and interactive way to practice identifying stress patterns.

Of course, this doesn't have to be an actual quiz—you can simply use quizzing platforms as a great way to give students immediate feedback and reinforce their learning. Although different teachers may take various approaches to how they visualize stress marks, (dashes over letters, capitalizing stressed syllables, or even wrapping rubber bands around their fingers and stretching the rubber band wide when they hit the stress), I'll suggest the use of the "small circle, big circle" method (o for unstressed, O for stressed). This makes it easy for both teachers and students to visually and audibly grasp the concept and separate the stressed sounds from the words themselves. They're also pretty easy to type into any keyboard.

ISTE STANDARDS
1.1.c / 1.3.b / 1.7.b

RESOURCES
brentgwarner.com/astressfullquiz

PRONUNCIATION

Activity Outline

Setup

- Choose a list of multisyllabic words to quiz on.

- Set up a quiz on the chosen platform using the "small circle, big circle" method (e.g., "supermarket": a) Oooo b) oOoo c) ooOo d) oooO). I've provided a sample in the resources, but you may prefer a different platform.

- If you have access to a premium quizzing platform, record and upload audio so students can listen to the stress pronunciation and practice on their own time.

Encourage students to dabble in the silly joy of mis-stressed words. It may just sound like "wrong" pronunciation to some, but as students are learning it also helps to reinforce what the stress is supposed to sound like. Plus, we can all do with a few more laughs in our classes!

Most of the quizzing platforms have a premium upgrade that allows you to upload audio, creating opportunities for students to study on their own time. Peek at the pricing to see if an upgrade is worth it for you.

Activity

- Students join the quiz via their devices.

- If live, the teacher calls out each word; if self-paced, students listen to pre-recorded audio.

- Students select the correct stress pattern from multiple-choice options.

- Have fun with competitions, team play, speed, etc. as each platform has different ways to gamify the review process.

Teacher's Role

- Prepare the quiz with appropriate words and stress patterns.

- Guide students through the activity, providing examples and support as needed.

  - Playing the role of sports announcer here is always a fun way to get students involved. As scores come rolling in, build up anticipation with playful banter: "Ali's in the lead right now, but I see Maria getting ready for a sneak attack … !"

- If appropriate, pause the game to clarify questions that the class as a whole struggled with.

Reflection

- Discuss common mistakes and clarify misunderstandings.

- Have students practice speaking the words with the correct stress in pairs or small groups.

Extensions

- Use this method for different pronunciation features, such as intonation or vowel sounds.
- Swapping out the small circles and big circles for words spelled out but with the schwa /ə/ can be a fun variation.

Materials/Tools

There are many quizzing platforms out there, and I regularly swap between them as features get updated. At this point, many students are familiar with platforms like Kahoot.com or Quizizz.com, so onboarding them can be quite easy. On the other hand, be careful that you don't overuse them as I have (occasionally) seen eyes roll from students who have to do them in every class.

If you want to expand your repertoire, consider using Gimkit.com as an alternative. It has a lot of interesting gamified elements and is based around them winning pretend, virtual money that they can then use to purchase upgrades and power-ups. It may get a little complicated for some, but for others it can add some strategy and planning that keeps them engaged.

For those who don't have access to the premium features of some of these platforms, Google Forms (forms.google.com) does allow for you to upload audio in the form of YouTube videos. It will take a bit of time to prep and link all the videos, but once you have them, you have them, and you can use them for other purposes as well.

CROSSSOUND PUZZLE

Students practice phonetic transcription and listening skills using the International Phonetic Alphabet (IPA) in a crossword puzzle format.

ISTE STANDARDS
1.1.a / 1.1.d / 1.2.b /
1.4.b / 1.6.d

RESOURCES
brentgwarner.com/
crosssoundpuzzle

Introduction

The CrossSound Puzzle is an innovative twist on traditional crossword puzzles designed to enhance students' understanding of phonetic transcription using the International Phonetic Alphabet (IPA). This activity combines the familiarity of crossword puzzles with the challenge of matching sounds instead of letters. By focusing on phonetic sounds, students will improve their pronunciation and listening skills, which are crucial for mastering any language. Additionally, this activity can incorporate audio clues, allowing students to hear the words and match them to their IPA symbols. This auditory element supports different learning styles and reinforces the connection between sounds and their phonetic representations.

Activity Outline

Setup

- Introduce students to the IPA chart and have students begin to familiarize themselves with the IPA letters and sounds.

- Prepare a list of vocabulary words and their IPA transcriptions.

- Create the crossword puzzle either by hand or by using an online generator, ensuring that crossing spaces match IPA symbols with the same sounds.

    - I recommend providing all the symbols that students will use in the slide deck as drag-and-drop items. This makes it so they aren't responsible for accessing unusual keyboards or symbol menus. It also helps provide minor clues as they will have a sense of the symbols they've already used.

- Record audio clips for each word to be used as clues.

- Make a copy of the puzzle page without an answer key and distribute it to students.

Activity

- Review/preview sounds and symbols with students. You can also use Sound Symbol Memory Match either as homework or a preview to warm students up.
- Students access the digital crossword puzzle.
- They listen to the audio clues provided by the teacher.
- Students drag and drop the IPA symbols provided into the appropriate squares.
- Students can check their answers with the teacher or compare answers with classmates.

Teacher's Role

- Prepare and upload the crossword puzzle and audio clues.
- Guide students through a review of the IPA chart and pronunciation practice.
- Monitor progress and provide feedback as necessary.
- Facilitate a class discussion on challenging sounds and common errors.

Reflection

- Encourage students to challenge the sounds they hear in the words. Many times, pronunciations may be different either regionally or generationally. If they disagree with a sound or have heard it pronounced a different way, open the conversation to the fluidity of pronunciation.

Extensions

- To make things more challenging, consider providing students only with audio recordings of the words, but with no information about where each word belongs in the puzzle. (See version B in the online resources.)
- Encourage students to try to capture their own pronunciation of the words using Say It Right.
- Students can create their own CrossSound Puzzles using new vocabulary words and share them with classmates. (In this case, even two or three crossing words would be a good challenge.)

There are endless variations here for the creative and adventurous souls out there! Instead of providing students with the IPA symbols to drag and drop into the puzzle, consider giving them audio files of each individual sound. If you want to make it easier, you could provide the first symbol of each row and column, or give students the crossing sound symbol. Want to make it even harder? Instead of giving students the words, give them clues so they first have to figure out what the word is, then transcribe it into IPA. As always, your creativity is the limit!

PRONUNCIATION

Materials/Tools

Note that while you can create this type of activity online using a crossword puzzle generator like PuzzleFast.com or CrosswordLabs.com, you'll need to double check that the puzzle maker can use IPA symbols. As you can imagine around IPA, there's a whole world of fonts and custom keyboard extensions to play with. If this is a rabbit hole you're ready to go down, you can start with installing the Charis SIL IPA font, which is linked to in the online resources. For those who are just trying to test the waters or only want to build one puzzle for their students, you may find that planning it out using good old pen and paper is a less overwhelming option.

If you want to record your own voice, tools like Audacity (audacityteam.org) or Vocaroo.com are great choices to record and share audio clips for the clues.

Draft. Sketch. Scribble. This Spot's for You!

A-MAZE-ING
EM-PHA-SIS

Students will improve their understanding of sentence intonation and emphasis by navigating a maze based on audio cues.

Introduction

Understanding intonation and emphasis in spoken language is crucial for English language learners as it affects the meaning and clarity of communication. aMAZEing emPHAsis is a fun and engaging activity that has them work their way through a simple maze using audio cues to determine their next move. The activity is designed to help students practice identifying intonation and stress, emphasizing how they can change the meaning of a sentence even when the words remain the same. Students can listen for the correct pronunciation and practice how each sentence might be spoken differently to imply a different meaning or focus. This activity can be done live in the classroom or assigned as homework for students to complete on their own time.

Activity Outline

Setup

- Review stress and emphasis in sentences.
- Provide students with the pre-designed interactive digital maze.
- Explain the rules of the maze and how intonation can change the direction they should move.

Activity

- Students listen to the first audio cue and identify the emphasized word or phrase in the sentence.

ISTE STANDARDS
1.1.c / 1.1.d / 1.3.b / 1.4.d / 1.5.c / 1.6.b

RESOURCES
brentgwarner.com/
amazeingemphasis

PRONUNCIATION

- Students move in the direction indicated by the meaning derived from the stressed word.
  - For example, "Have YOU been to Brussels?" versus "Have you been to BRUSSELS?" where the first is focused on the listener (as compared, possibly, to another person in the group that we already established has been to Brussels) and the second is focused on the location (as compared, possibly, to another city in Europe).
- Repeat for the remaining sentences until reaching the final marker on the maze.

Teacher's Role

- Introduce the concept of intonation, stress, and emphasis in sentences.
- Provide examples and model how to interpret the meaning based on the emphasized word.
- Monitor student progress, providing guidance and feedback as needed.
- Evaluate students' paths through the maze to confirm whether they assessed the emphases correctly.

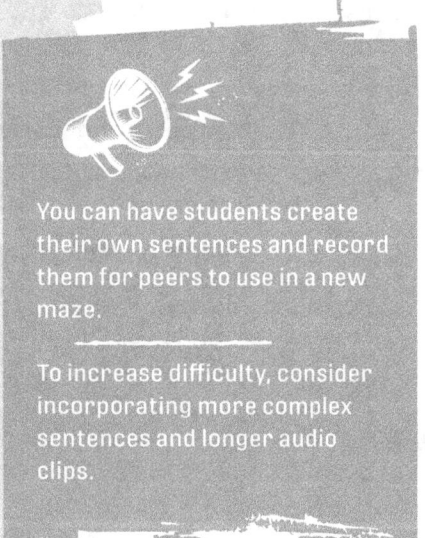

You can have students create their own sentences and record them for peers to use in a new maze.

To increase difficulty, consider incorporating more complex sentences and longer audio clips.

Reflection

- Students can discuss the final position on their maze with peers, explaining their reasoning for each move. In pairs or small groups, they can listen in to see where they diverged from one another and whether they can come to a consensus on the right sounds.

Extensions

- Students can add audio clips to the maze to indicate what the sentence should sound like if it is meant to imply a different meaning on the maze.
- The basic concept behind this activity can be widely adapted to all sorts of different games. For example, you can find different ways to emphasize a sentence and use each emphasis point as a cardinal direction to move across a tiled board.
  - When(up) do you(down) think Elena(left)will move(right)?
  - When: We know/agree that Elena will move, but knowing the time is important.
  - You: I've told you when I think she'll move, now I want to know what you think.

PRONUNCIATION

- Elena: We already discussed someone else who will move, now let's discuss Elena.
- Move: We've discussed other things about Elena, but now I want to know specifically about her moving.

○ You could then use different versions of the same sentence to indicate to students which way they should move across the board. They could also be challenged to make their own recordings to show that they can produce the stresses necessary for each implied meaning.

Materials/Tools

This activity can be built in any slide deck or online whiteboard that allows you to insert audio. This includes Google Slides (slides.google.com), Microsoft PowerPoint (powerpoint.office.com), and other generally robust platforms. If you want to move into the Extensions to build production skills on top of recognition skills, I recommend FigJam (figma.com/figjam). While other platforms have hinted at the technology coming, FigJam has a Widgets section that allows users to record voice memos directly onto the board.

Notes, Sketches, Brain Dumps Welcome Here

EDTECH FOR MULTILINGUAL LEARNERS

THE ISTE STUDENT STANDARDS

1.1: Empowered Learner

Students leverage technology to take an active role in choosing, achieving and demonstrating competency in their learning goals, informed by the learning sciences.

1.1.a Learning Goals

Students set learning goals, develop strategies leveraging technology to achieve them and reflect on the learning process to improve learning outcomes.

1.1.b Customized Learning Environments

Students build networks and customize their learning environments in ways that support the learning process.

1.1.c Feedback to Improve Practice

Students use technology to seek feedback that informs and improves their practice and to demonstrate their learning in a variety of ways.

1.1.d Technology Fundamentals

Students understand fundamental concepts of how technology works, demonstrate the ability to choose and use current technologies effectively, and are adept at thoughtfully exploring emerging technologies.

1.2: Digital Citizen

Students recognize the responsibilities and opportunities for contributing to their digital communities.

1.2.a Digital Footprint

Students manage their digital identity and understand the lasting impact of their online behaviors on themselves and others and make safe, legal and ethical decisions in the digital world.

1.2.b Online Interactions

Students demonstrate empathetic, inclusive interactions online and use technology to responsibly contribute to their communities.

1.2.c Safeguard Well-being

Students safeguard their well-being by being intentional about what they do online and how much time they spend online.

1.2.d Digital Privacy

Students take action to protect their digital privacy on devices and manage their personal data and security while online.

1.3: Knowledge Constructor

Students critically curate a variety of resources using digital tools to construct knowledge, produce creative artifacts and make meaningful learning experiences for themselves and others.

1.3.a Effective Research Strategies

Students use effective research strategies to find resources that support their learning needs, personal interests and creative pursuits.

1.3.b Evaluate Information

Students evaluate the accuracy, validity, bias, origin, and relevance of digital content.

1.3.c Curate Information

Students curate information from digital resources using a variety of tools and methods to create collections of artifacts that demonstrate meaningful connections or conclusions.

1.3.d Explore Real-World Issues

Students build knowledge by actively exploring real-world issues and problems, developing ideas and theories, and pursuing answers and solutions.

1.4: Innovative Designer

Students use a variety of technologies within a design process to identify and solve problems by creating new, useful or imaginative solutions.

1.4.a Design Process

Students know and use a deliberate design process for generating ideas, testing theories, creating innovative artifacts or solving authentic problems.

1.4.b Design Constraints

Students select and use digital tools to plan and manage a design process that considers design constraints and calculated risks.

1.4.c Prototypes

Students develop, test and refine prototypes as part of a cyclical design process.

1.4.d Open-Ended Problems

Students exhibit a tolerance for ambiguity, perseverance and the capacity to work with open-ended problems

1.5: Computational Thinker

Students develop and employ strategies for understanding and solving problems in ways that leverage the power of technological methods to develop and test solutions.

1.5.a Problem Definitions

Students formulate problem definitions suited for technology-assisted methods such as data analysis, abstract models and algorithmic thinking in exploring and finding solutions.

1.5.b Data Sets

Students collect data or identify relevant data sets, use digital tools to analyze them and represent data in various ways to facilitate problem-solving and decision-making.

1.5.c Decompose Problems

Students break problems into component parts, extract key information and develop descriptive models to understand complex systems or facilitate problem-solving.

1.5.d Algorithmic Thinking

Students understand how automation works and use algorithmic thinking to develop a sequence of steps to create and test automated solutions.

1.6: Creative Communicator

Students communicate clearly and express themselves creatively for a variety of purposes using the platforms, tools, styles, formats and digital media appropriate to their goals.

1.6.a Choose Platforms or Tools

Students choose the appropriate platforms and digital tools for meeting the desired objectives of their creation or communication.

1.6.b Original and Remixed Works

Students create original works or responsibly repurpose or remix digital resources into new creations.

1.6.c Communicate Comple Ideas
Students use digital tools to visually communicate comple ideas to others.

1.6.d Customize the Message
Students publish or present content that customizes the message and medium for their intended audiences.

1.7: Global Collaborator
Students use digital tools to broaden their perspectives and enrich their learning by collaborating with others and working effectively in teams locally and globally.

1.7.a Global Connections
Students use digital tools to connect with peers from a variety of backgrounds recognizing diverse viewpoints and broadening mutual understanding.

1.7.b Multiple Viewpoints
Students use collaborative technologies to work with others, including peers, experts and community members, to eamine issues and problems from multiple viewpoints.

1.7.c Project Teams
Students contribute constructively to project teams, assuming various roles and responsibilities to work effectively toward a common goal.

1.7.d Local and Global Issues
Students explore local and global issues, and use collaborative technologies to work with others to investigate solutions.

BIBLIOGRAPHY

Front Materials

Bergson-Shilcock, A., Taylor, R., & Hodge, N. (2023, February 6). *Closing the Digital Skill Divide*. National Skills Coalition. https://nationalskillscoalition.org/wp-content/uploads/2023/02/NSC-DigitalDivide_report_Feb2023.pdf

Blass, L., & Tolnai, C. (2019). *Power Up Your Classroom*. International Society for Technology in Education.

Brown, G. (1990). *Listening to Spoken English* (2nd ed.). Taylor & Francis. (Original work published 1977)

National Center for Education Statistics. (2024). English Learners in Public Schools. *Condition of Education*. U.S. Department of Education, Institute of Education Sciences. Retrieved 01/19/2025, from https://nces.ed.gov/programs/coe/indicator/cgf.

Stock, J. (2020). *Awesome Sauce*. International Society for Technology in Education.

Thorn, S. (2021). *Integrating Authentic Listening into the Language Classroom*. Pavilion Publishing.

Underhill, A. (2005). *Sound Foundations: Learning and Teaching Pronunciation*. Macmillan ELT.

Ur, P. (1984). *Teaching listening comprehension*. Cambridge University Press.

U.S. Department of Education, Office of Planning, Evaluation and Policy Development, Policy and Program Studies Service. (2019). Supporting English learners through technology: What districts and teachers say about digital learning resources for English learners: Results in brief. https://www.ed.gov/sites/ed/files/rschstat/eval/title-iii/180414-dlr-results-in-brief.pdf

Webb, S. (2007). The effects of synonymy on second-language vocabulary learning. *Reading in a Foreign Language, 19*(2). https://files.eric.ed.gov/fulltext/EJ777733.pdf

ISTE Standards for Students by Activity

	1.1.a	1.1.b	1.1.c	1.1.d	1.2.a	1.2.b	1.2.c	1.2.d	1.3.a	1.3.b	1.3.c	1.3.d
Jeopardistinctions			○									
Transcription Tracker	○							○				
Podcast Explorer's Log	○	○										○
Whaddyaeer			○					○		○		
Lyric Lover		○					○		○	○		
Sketch & Guess			○			○						
Orderly Listening				○					○	○		
Behind the Curtains												
Voice Vibe			○									
Opinion Quest										○		○
De-Silent Films	○			○				○				
Fiberoptic Fishbowl Forum			○	○			○			○		
Podcast Pulse	○							○				○
AI Chatterbox	○							○				
Deb(AI)te Practice	○							○				
Role Play Roulette			○									
Storyboard Scenes		○		○		○					○	
Drawn to Reading	○	○		○						○		○
Social Readia		○	○		○	○				○		○
Trending Takeaways			○	○	○	○				○		○
Custom Extensive Readers		○		○								
Paragraph Puzzle				○						○		
Character Chat		○	○							○	○	
Long Reading Snowball	○	○	○									

EDTECH FOR MULTILINGUAL LEARNERS

1.4.a	1.4.b	1.4.c	1.4.d	1.5.a	1.5.b	1.5.c	1.5.d	1.6.a	1.6.b	1.6.c	1.6.d	1.7.a	1.7.b	1.7.c	1.7.d
						○							○	○	
	○							○			○		○		
						○		○							○
						○									
						○					○				
									○		○				
									○	○					
		○				○					○			○	
		○									○				
		○				○					○				
○								○			○				
											○		○		
								○					○		
○											○			○	
○								○			○		○		
		○				○							○		
								○	○		○				
	○								○	○					
						○				○	○				
								○	○	○	○	○			
									○						
		○	○												
		○									○		○		
									○		○				

Continued

	1.1.a	1.1.b	1.1.c	1.1.d	1.2.a	1.2.b	1.2.c	1.2.d	1.3.a	1.3.b	1.3.c	1.3.d
Make a Meme		●		●			●					
Snap 'n' Scribble	●					●						
A Rose by Any Other N(AI)m							●					
CollaborEssays	●	●	●							●		
Newsroom Bloggers	●		●			●		●	●	●	●	●
Reverse Analysis Revision	●		●							●		
Automated Ideation	●	●		●					●	●	●	
Unusual Pairings	●	●		●	●				●	●	●	●
Synonym Searcher		●								●	●	
Idiomaginative Explorations			●	●		●		●		●		
ChatVCB		●	●	●						●		
The Infinite Content Bot	●	●								●		●
Magic Picture Dictionary		●		●		●					●	
Phrasal Frenzy			●							●		
Corpus Clash			●						●	●		
Antonyms on a Log			●	●				●		●		●
Words in the Wild		●		●	●	●						●
Investigated, Used, and Discussed			●	●		●						
Sound Symbol Memory Match			●	●						●		
Minimal Pairs Cascade	●		●			●						
Say It Right			●							●		
Speak and See			●			●				●		
A Stress-Full Quiz			●							●		
CrossSound Puzzle	●			●		●						
aMAZEing emPHAsis			●	●						●		

1.4.a	1.4.b	1.4.c	1.4.d	1.5.a	1.5.b	1.5.c	1.5.d	1.6.a	1.6.b	1.6.c	1.6.d	1.7.a	1.7.b	1.7.c	1.7.d
								○	○						
			○						○		○	○	○		
			○						○		○				
									○		○		○	○	
											○		○		○
			○												
			○												
								○							
					○						○				
○						○			○		○				
		○		○		○									
									○	○	○				
											○		○		
					○						○				
									○	○	○		○		
											○				
						○									
									○						
									○					○	
													○		
	○										○				
			○			○			○						

Your Turn—What Would You Add?

EDTECH FOR MULTILINGUAL LEARNERS

INDEX

Write or Draw Your Own Ideas Here

EDTECH FOR MULTILINGUAL LEARNERS

Transform Instruction to
Transform Students' Lives

Our Transformational Learning Principles (TLPs) are evidence-based practices that ensure students have access to high-impact, joyful learning experiences.

Endorsed by AASA and NASSP, the TLPs provide a shared language and a framework for reimagining teaching and learning, focusing on nurturing student growth, guiding intellectual curiosity, and empowering learners to take ownership of their education.

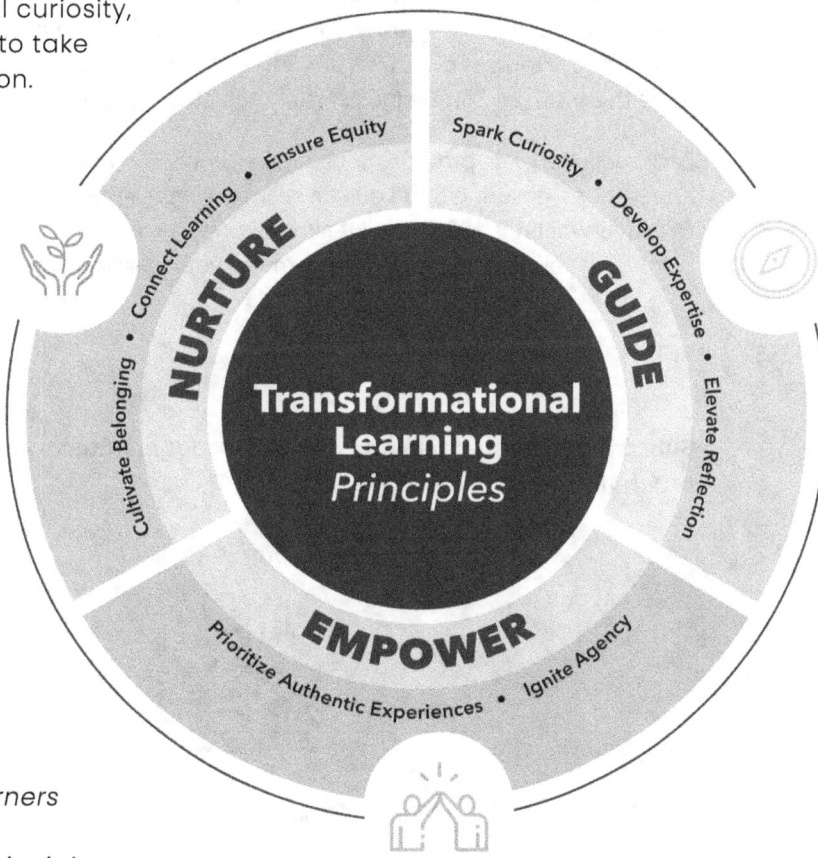

Edtech for Multilingual Learners relates to many of the Transformation Learning Principles, including Connect Learning and Ignite Agency.

Learn more at **iste.org/tlps**

EXPAND WHAT YOU'VE LEARNED FROM THIS BOOK!

Check Out the ELT Toolkit:
Edtech for Teaching Excellence

You've discovered powerful strategies in *Edtech for Multilingual Learners*—now put them directly into action with the ELT Toolkit, written by Brent Warner as a supplement to this book and hosted by TESOL International Association. The ELT Toolkit is a practical companion for teachers who don't have time to keep on top of all of the resources out there, and instead offers clear, hands-on guidance for more than 100 (and growing!) carefully selected edtech tools.

Each resource page provides concise overviews and real-world classroom applications, ensuring that you can seamlessly turn theory into practice without tech overwhelm. The ELT Toolkit allows you to save time and energy while extending your learning and transforming your classroom engagement.

Subscribe today and take the guesswork out of edtech, so you can focus on what you do best: teaching!

tesol.org/elt-toolkit